Butterfly Travels

"We delight in the beauty of the butterfly,
but rarely admit the changes it has gone through
to achieve that beauty."
~ Maya Angelou

by Jennifer Watson
illustrated by Elizabeth Hamby

Butterfly Travels

© 2014 by Jennifer Watson
Cover Artwork © 2014 by Elizabeth Hamby

ISBN-13: 978-0692333808
Printed in the United States of America

All rights reserved. The text of this publication, or any part thereof, may not be reproduced in any manner whatsoever without written permission from the author.

10 9 8 7 6 5 4 3 2 1

Disclaimer: This book is based on true events. The author has tried to recreate events, locales and conversations from memories of them. In order to maintain their anonymity wherever possible, names and identifying details have been omitted.

With Love and Gratitude

For Samantha and Bryan: The best adventure of my life. You are my heart, my life, my soul. Thank you for teaching me unconditional love and making me want to be a better person. There is no greater blessing in life than having you as my children. Thank you for choosing me to be your mommy xo.

For my parents: Thank you for raising me to be independent and for encouraging me to always go after my dreams. I finally did it—I wrote my first book! I love you. You both inspired me in your own ways, and I am thankful you gave me life. Mom, thank you for being my rock, and for being the safe place to always come home to after my adventures are over.

For my sisters: Up for another adventure? God blessed me with the best sisters a girl could have. Thank you for sticking by me through thick and thin (and fat and skinny, happy and sad, crazy and sane…you get it ;-)).

For my family, friends, loves of past and present, and acquaintances: Thank you for the inspiration, the support and the lessons. Every connection is a treasure. Whether you know it or not, you <u>all</u> made an impact on me. May you cherish all of your connections and adventures.

A Note About My "Characters"

These are real events in my life and real people who accompanied me on my adventures at different stages in my life. I have chosen not to name names specifically, but certain identities may be assumed. This memoir is a representation of my experience, my perspective, my feelings, and my journey, and in no way is the complete representation of any other individual.

There are two sides to every story, and my dialogues about my adventures and the people in them in no way reflect upon their true, whole, beautiful character, but rather, my interaction with them at the time from my point of view. Every person in my life has been a blessing. Even in the heartache there was love, and for every human perceived flaw in another, I discovered an equal flaw in myself. In no way was this book designed to hurt anyone or misrepresent them in any way. It is just a reflection of my life, my stories, my experiences, my lessons, and my healing. If you are indirectly referenced in this book in any way, it is because you contributed to my life in a profound way, and I have much love, gratitude and respect for your role in making me who I am today.

To everyone who touched my life: I love and honor you. Thank you for being with me on this journey.

The Adventures

Introduction	7
The Emergent Traveler	9
1. Where Did the Love Begin?	11
2. A Day at the Races: Saratoga Springs	15
3. "I Don't See any Buffalo"	19
4. Indian Cavern Crisis	23
5. Cousin Love: Navigating Puberty in New Jersey	27
6. Over (and Into) the Frost Valley River	31
7. Lake Adventure: Treasured Summers	35
8. Toronto Tunes: A Soulmate Discovered	39
9. Great Adventure and My First Kiss	43
10. Virginia & All that Jazz: Confessions of a Teenage Heartbreak	47
11. The Winds of College: From Hershey to Lancaster	51
12. Falling for Fell's Point, Baltimore	55
13. An Introduction to Fame: The Philly Arena	59
14. A New Home, A New Me: My Barcelona Life	63
15. I Left My Heart in Europe	67
16. A London Proposal	73
17. A Sales Girl on the Road: My Trade Show Excursions	77
18. Dad and Disney: Hide the Kona Coffee	83
19. Tracing My Irish Roots	87
20. Who Moved My Chi Chi? A Hawaiian Getaway	91
21. A Dry Spell and a Dry Heart	95
22. To Saturn and Back: An Energetic Journey	101
Saturn Rain	104

23. Sisterly Bonds at the Jersey Shore 107
24. What Happens in Atlantic City, Doesn't Always Stay There (Part 1) 111
25. Owning my Loneliness: Bahama Seclusion............................115
26. A Summit of Soulmates: A Californian Beginning................121
27. Bonding Time at Rockin' Horse Ranch 127
28. Into the Woods: Our First Camping Experience....................133
29. My Vegan Thanksgiving in San Diego.....................................139
30. A Defining Moment: My Graduation in Miami.....................145
31. What Happens in Atlantic City, Doesn't Always Stay There (Part 2) 149
32. Disney Cruising with the Family 153
33. Home is Where the Heart Heals: A NYC Experience 159
34. Up, Up and Away…in a Hot Air Balloon 165
35. Life in the Afterglow: A Sedona Awakening..........................169
36. The Renaissance Fair: Unleashing my Inner Princess...........175
37. A New England Escape 179
My Escape 188
Epilogue: Where to Next?...191

Introduction

I've come to realize that every adventure I've ever been on has been a deeper awakening to who I am. They have been more profound in recent years, but as far back as I can remember, every time I left my home for a vacation, short visit or business trip, a deeper purpose was revealed. I feel it comes from just letting loose outside of the comforts of my life; to be who I am as I understand how other people or cultures work; to explore hurts that come up, or messages I receive, or simply new friendships that are formed.

I find myself moved with each journey. I think that is why I love traveling so much. Some people travel to escape. Not me. (Not usually.) I travel to explore, expand, learn and uncover truths. It's like I am a pirate searching for treasure or a frontiersman seeking new land. But cuter and more heart-based. *Wink*

All throughout my life, I have documented these journeys in some way—whether through my childhood diary, a photo montage detailing every moment, a personal journal or a blog. And then after writing one particular blog, it dawned on me that my life's journey would make an excellent compilation for a book.

Not because I am special or different from anyone else. Not because I went on extraordinary adventures that people could only dream of experiencing. On the contrary: it is my ordinary self, traveling to many common places others reading this have most likely visited themselves. It is the story of an everyday girl, finding her way, healing her heart and opening new doors to what life could be—a girl that everyone can relate to. A girl (or person) very much like yourself, perhaps.

And that's why I am sharing my adventures. There are not a lot of people out there to relate to on a personal level. There are the icons that we look up to that if we met in person, we would be starstruck. There are the spiritual leaders out there who channel from "ascended masters" with profound messages of divine guidance. There are the experts with extensive education in the classroom and in the world who illuminate our intellect.

And then there are people like me. Like your sister, your mother, your grandmother, your neighbor, your teacher, your librarian—your everyday, beautiful community member. Your reflection.

May you go on your own adventures as you read about mine—literally and figuratively. And may this open a door for you to feel safe to explore who you are, love who you are and share who you are with the world. Because "ordinary" as we all are, being true to ourselves is what makes each of us also "extra"ordinary.

Blessings, light and love,

The Emergent Traveler

Sit still my little one, where are you going now?
I'm off on an adventure!

The high seas are calling me to find their buried treasure
The princesses are calling me to attend their ball
The pyramids are calling me to unravel their mystery
The beaches are calling me to build their biggest sandcastle
The mountains are calling me to hike their steepest rocks
The forests are calling me to run wild with their animals
The cities are calling me to dazzle in their lights
The universe is calling me to play in its abundance

Can't you see, there is so much to see?
To explore, to uncover, to learn?
The world is a pretty big place, and I need to see it all

I need to dip my toes into the bluest of waters
I need to find the rarest of precious stones
I need to see the most colorful of landscapes
I need to hear the quirkiest voice of all animals
I need to smell the prettiest of flowers
I need to taste the most peculiar of foods
I need to sense the profoundest of spirit

It's okay, I will never go too far
As to never know where my home is
For I love the here as much as the there
But wherever spirit leads me to go, is where I shall follow

And so I must follow my heart into the unknown
I must break free from this cocoon and fly, fly away
To see the world through a butterfly's eyes

1. Where Did it All Begin?

I'm not quite sure where my love of travel came from, to be honest. I can't pinpoint an exact moment where I said — how fun! I want to do this more! I just think it's been in my blood, in my DNA, since the moment I was created. My first overnight adventure was to Lake George when I was three years old with my parents and grandparents. We stayed in a little cabin near the water and traveled to local attractions. Obviously, I don't remember it, but my mother said that even back then, I showed a thirst for being on an adventure, and I didn't mind being away from home; I adjusted just fine.

She said I was a very quiet child, taking it all in. We went to the North Pole to visit Santa Claus, which she said I loved. We also explored Magicland, where I was enamored with all of the fairy-tale characters. (Go figure — I am not surprised, as a Disney aficionado, Renaissance lover and all around wannabe princess.) She said I also enjoyed going down to the water to go fishing with my dad, but wasn't a big fan of the Fort. Clearly, even at the tender age of three, I wasn't a big fan of traditional history.

Although I do not remember it cerebrally, there is something that keeps calling me back to see where it all began. And it's a nod to the type of traveler that I am: I seek adventures with places that feel close to my heart, not necessarily the "must sees" of the world, although I am sure those are wonderful experiences as well. When I let my heart guide me to my explorations, I am

> *Looking back on my journeys, I can see that every single one held a message for me.*

never led astray. I remember when I planned my Euro-trip, I yearned to see Switzerland, and added in Paris "just because." And both experiences certainly remain memorable ones.

When I first incepted the idea for this book, I had no idea of the places I have already traveled to—or how often I did. Wow, I must have been a happy little nomad in a past life somewhere. I do love having a home to come back to. I definitely am content being rooted in a safe, loving haven. But I do also adore being on the go, exploring, learning new things. I have a deep, deep respect for other cultures: their language, their arts, their customs. I honor how others live and what they believe. It's what guided me to major in International Business to begin with.

Funny aside: when asked what I wanted my college major to be (note: not what I wanted to be when I grew up) all I could respond with is: something where I can wear pretty business suits and travel the world. So when International Business popped up on my radar, it seemed to be the perfect fit. And in many ways, it was. I had an amazing, once-in-a-lifetime opportunity to study abroad, and lived in Barcelona, Spain for six blessed, life-changing months. It was a dream come true. (Although not dressed in suits, I learned some new fashion and sported it, which worked just as well!)

So as I created an outline about my adventures for my story, I was surprised by the number of chapters—the number of adventures—I have taken over the course of my 39 years. I knew I had a decent amount under my belt, but I had no idea how travel was truly a part of my life. It's proven to be a foundation for creating who I was, and for understanding others.

Jennifer Watson

A few years back, when I really began to study the innerworkings of astrology and my own chart, a mentor pointed out that my spiritual blueprint was all about adventure. For you astro junkies —I have Jupiter in Aries in the 9th house: a natural explorer, student, teacher and traveler; a lover of knowledge and wisdom; a seeker of all things curious. Once I heard that this was true to who I was, and that there was nothing wrong with me for always wanting to take a "vacation" somewhere, I embraced it wholeheartedly. It felt so right. It all made sense.

Looking back on my journeys, I can see that every single one held a message for me. Sometimes it was just as simple as appreciating those with me. Other times, it was a ground-breaking transformation leading closer to the truth of who I was. All were beautiful; even the difficult ones. So I share my experiences with you with love, truth and trust.

And although there are many chapters in this book, and many adventures, I kept them short. I didn't feel the need to function as a travel agent and sell you on why or why not you should visit a particular place. It's not about the specifics of where I was and what was around me and who I met—unless they aided as part of the grander story. It's about the journey, the lessons, the transformations, and the experiences. Buckle up, readers—you are about to take a roller coaster ride through my life. All I ask is that you sit in the front seat with me, and raise those hands up for every twist, drop and loop-de-loop you feel that resonates with you.

Let the adventure begin!

2. A Day at the Races: Saratoga Springs

Saratoga Springs. My first full memory of a trip. I was 5 years old, not too long after the birth of my sister, and the summer before I entered first grade. I had a difficult time adjusting to being a big sister. After all, I was the one and only child around for 5 years. Not even my older cousins were nearby. So, that summer I left for Saratoga Springs with my Nanny and Poppy (my mother's parents) to visit some family—a break somehow my parents and grandparents knew I needed to feel a little special again.

We stayed with some relatives in their summer home. I can still remember exactly what it looked like: the light that shone in through the windows; the kitchen table where I was introduced to Cookie Crisp cereal for the first time; the living room where I slept and "secretly" stayed up late to watch Friday Night Videos. I still remember every song and video that was on that night, and even to this day, whenever I hear them, they always remind me of this particular vacation.

I felt like I was a "big girl" and not a baby anymore. Not because I was forced to grow up and be the big sister. Not because I was now in school and had to be more responsible. But because I was given opportunities to explore new things. (Trust me, trying a cereal made entirely of "cookies" is a mind-blowing treat when you are five!) Staying up late way past my bedtime, watching "grown-up" tv with older family cousins and having a sleepover party were all new to me—and I cherished every part of it. I was becoming my own little person, one who was free to try new things and ask questions and be my curious self.

My Nanny and Poppy were big supporters of my curiosity. That's not to say my parents weren't, but their job was to make sure I had all my needs met, a good education, learn right from wrong, and teach me a whole bunch of important lessons I now understand as a mother myself. A grandparent has the freedom to look outside of the normal parental responsibilities and help guide a young child's dreams—and they both did an outstanding job. It didn't hurt that they both loved adventures themselves, and inspired me with their own tales of travels. I could sit for hours drinking tea with my Nanny while she shared all of her stories.

So it should come as no surprise that they tried to expose me to new experiences while we were in Saratoga. Some I was game for—some I was not. I remember Poppy telling me that we could go out fishing on the lake. I thought that was the coolest idea in the world! I loved to go fishing with my father, but it was always from the docks, and never on the water. I remember thinking I wanted to catch the biggest fish ever for my Daddy. God bless my grandfather and his love for me: he spent $50 to get a fishing/boating license for that trip, found a boat, and walked me all the way down to the lake. He put on my life preserver and had the fishing gear all ready—and what did I do? I started crying hysterically because I didn't want to go in the water anymore. I was afraid that I would drown and die. My little 5-year-old self just couldn't do it.

My Poppy, true to form, didn't even flinch. He was a kind, gentle man. He had gone through a lot of trouble to get that license (though at the time, I had no understanding of that) but he didn't even try to force me. He asked if I was sure, but when he saw that the fear ran deep, he just packed everything up, gave me a pat on the head and said, "Let's go back home and do something else."

> *I was becoming my own little person, one who was free to try new things and ask questions and be my curious self.*

I think that was my first memory of true compassion. I always felt love and affection and many other warm and fuzzy emotions from my family. But that was the first time that I recall being in a state of fear, and being told simply that it was okay, and wasn't judged for it or pressured. I didn't even know at the time that I "should have" felt guilty over the whole situation. All I knew then was that my Poppy loved me enough to take me to the lake, and then to take me away from it. That's all that mattered in my little head.

That debacle out on the lake didn't stop them from still going on another adventure, though. I remember with fond memories being brought to the racetrack to see the horses race against each other. I remember the newspaper-like flyers with the names of the horses on them and Poppy asking me to pick a name I liked. Then he would go up to the window and bet on the horse I picked. Although I was young, I understood the basic concept that I was trying to guess which horse would win, and if it did, then Poppy got a prize. And I do believe I won him his $50 back.

I can still remember the whole trip with such vividness. The quaintness of the tiny house that brought many families together under one roof in love. The laughter of the adults as they played cards late into the night. The smell of the salty air down by the lake and feeling the wind as it blew up sand from the dirt road path. The thrill of watching where my horses placed in each race, wondering if I picked the right one. The smiles of my grandparents as they shared this wonderful experience with me, and restored my sense of importance within my family. I went home a happier girl—ready to welcome the new baby into the family and finally take on my role as the big sister.

3. "I Don't See Any Buffalo"

Most of my childhood adventures included my maternal grandparents, who lived with us most of our lives. My paternal grandparents lived in Buffalo, NY, and it was rare that we had a chance to see them. I think that is why this particular trip holds a special place in my heart. I felt sad not knowing who these grandparents were. I would get cards and calls from them, and never for one moment did I doubt their love for me. But to be able to visit them and get to know them was something I remember being very excited about—more than the places that we planned to see when we got there. My aunt, uncle and cousins also lived there, and it was exciting to me to find out what it would be like to have a "big sister" instead of just be one.

Let me tell you—that was one long car ride. And with 3 young girls in the back seat, you bet it was a true-to-life "Are we there yet?" kind of trip. But it was also a fun experience for me, and I didn't mind it so much. We would play all kinds of games, like "I Spy", see how many states we can find with the other cars' license plates and find words on road signs for every letter of the alphabet. We read and colored and amused ourselves. And I am about to get all old school and say "back when I was young, we didn't have DVD players or Ipods to pass the time." Nope. We survived with what we had. We sang together as a family, told stories and made up games. To me, that is such a wonderful way to spend a car trip—because bonding happens when you interact with others, not when you do your own thing. And I have taken that

> *Here, it was out in the open, and for the first time, I was outside of my protective bubble.*

with me on road trips today. I try to stay present to those in my car and connect with them. I mean—what fun is it to ignore each other? I spying a license plate from Kansas was much more fun than taking a nap. But maybe that's just me!

I think what stands out the most about our road trip is my little sister and her innocent curiosity. As we drove towards our destination, she genuinely looked confused when my parents announced we had arrived in Buffalo at long last. Baffled, her curious little voice peeped up: "But Mommy, I don't see any Buffalo." To this day, that has to be the cutest thing my sister ever said. Not quite sure she ever understood that it was a place, and not a herd.

Once we arrived, it was a bit of a culture shock for me. I didn't get how somewhere else in New York, or even my family, could be so different from us. My cousin asked me if I wanted "Pop" and it took me quite some time to figure out that she meant soda. Beer was all around, and it flowed. As the daughter of a recovering alcoholic, that was something foreign to me. Alcohol wasn't even allowed at our family parties; it was forbidden out of respect for my dad and his commitment to sobriety. So it was very confusing to a young girl to witness people acting so funny, and getting in fights, all because of these glass bottles we couldn't drink out of.

I mean, I had some level of understanding from my earlier years when my dad wasn't in recovery, but it was hidden from me as much as possible. Here, it was out in the open, and for the first time, I was outside of my protective bubble. And I truly got then and there why we were so strict about alcohol in the house and at parties. It was not a pretty situation.

But in the daylight, things were different, and I had the chance to spend some alone time with my grandma. I remember going over to her house, right across the street from my aunt, and sitting with her in the swing that my grandfather built by hand. It was just me and her and we talked and talked for hours. I can't remember the conversation, but I could remember the feeling. It was the one and only time I remember being with her—I was only a one-year-old the first time—and I remember feeling this strong connection and this bond of love with her.

I adored her, and thought she was so beautiful. She had this perfect white hair (now I know it was a wig), bronzed, young-looking skin and very kind eyes. She was very gentle when she spoke to me, but I felt the strength of the woman she was inside. I will never forget that moment for as long as I live. I didn't need to see her everyday to know I was special—that all of us girls were special to her. Proximity didn't determine how much or how little we were loved; the heart did.

I don't remember much of my grandfather from this trip, but I do remember him from his visits to us after Grandma passed. I knew he was a hard worker, and that he had parts of his fingers cut off from an accident at work. I knew that he had tattoos on his toes that made me giggle as a younger child. And I remember him calling us "hunsy bunnies" as a term of affection. I didn't feel as close to him as I did to my grandmother, but I think that's only because I naturally gravitated towards the strong women of the family. Even then I knew I was just like them.

Not all of my family encounters were as pleasant, unfortunately. On this trip, I also met my official Godfather. I had high expectations; after all, I saw how my other uncle was so wonderful to my sister as her Godfather, so I thought now that he would see me in person, I would feel that bond that was missing in my life.

But I didn't. All I got was a "I will get you anything in the world you want. If you want a parrot, I will buy you a parrot."

I never did get that parrot. Or a card, or a phone call, or any kind of acknowledgement after that. I believe that was my first real heartbreak from a man. It hurt my heart on many levels. I was still just a child and didn't understand what I had done so wrong to make him not like me or want to be a part of my life. Was I not good enough, not pretty enough, not fun enough? It was hard for my young mind to grasp the complexities of human nature, and that there was much more to this story that had nothing to do with me.

Years later, I would learn he had passed, leaving me with this single memory of a man who was supposed to be one of my most special life guardians. By then, I had already come to terms with our lack of connection, and felt nothing but pity for a man who I heard had apparently led a very tragic life. Perspective and age are truly master conduits for compassion and healing.

Thankfully, the hurt I felt from my uncle's "rejection" on that trip was short-lived, as my parents took us to see Niagara Falls. I remember feeling awe-stricken by the falls and wanting to go over them in a barrel like they did in the cartoons. Obviously, that didn't happen. But we did get to explore Toronto and get a taste of Canada, and I remember thinking that seeing another country's money was the coolest thing ever. My first exposure to another world, and I loved every moment of it. I wanted to learn more, and was fascinated by it all.

Looking back on this particular trip is bittersweet. It gave me some beautiful and painful family memories that I will never forget. But it also opened up my love of exploring other cultures—and of road trips. And thanks to my little sis, it taught me that you can't take everything literally.

4. Indian Cavern Crisis

You never know how precious life is, or how much you take it for granted, until you are faced with a life-threatening situation. We took a family trip to Hershey, where we planned to go on wild rollercoasters (and my favorite chocolate-making ride) at Hershey Park, checking out the Amish country and fun factories in Lancaster and hitting up our favorite "family" buffet—just like we had done before and loved. But this time, life took an unexpected turn of events. It was a trip that we will all remember vividly for the rest out our lives.

We arrived in Hershey and checked into our hotel. We decided that after the long drive, we would hit up the park the next day, but we still wanted to do something since we were all so excited to be there. We had seen a sign for the Indian Echo Caverns, so my parents thought they would be really cool to explore and check out. So we went, and after being in intense heat all day, the cold dampness of the caverns was a shock to all of our systems. It was a boring exploration, and we were freezing. None of us enjoyed it, and we couldn't wait to get out and just get back to the hotel to rest up for our much more exciting adventure to come.

We were all snuggled up and ready for bed, and my sisters and I were already sleeping. All of a sudden, we heard a blood-curdling scream: my mother saw my youngest sister having a seizure. None of us knew what to do, and we were all petrified that she was going to die. My mother was panicked and paralyzed with fear. At the time, we didn't know that you were supposed to let a seizure run its course, and to just put her in a safe place until it stopped. My sister finally stopped seizing, but then was burning up with a fever. My dad immediately drew a bath to cool her down, while my other sister and I were told to go get help.

I will never forget the two of us running out in our nightgowns, banging on doors for help, trying to get the elevator to quickly go down to the front desk to call an ambulance for our little sister. We were so, so scared. As the oldest, I tried to be calm and brave as best as I could, but even I was in a state of shock over what was happening. The people at the front desk were nice but slow, and I remember somehow finding the clarity to tell them to get an ambulance fast and explained what happened. It was then that I (and my family) realized that I'm the one you can always count on to keep calm, take action and be the supportive rock to lean on in a crisis situation. A tough responsibility for someone to take on for the rest of her life, but it just became part of who I was from that point on.

We returned to the room after getting help, waiting for what felt like hours. My mother was at a loss of what to do, just cradling my sister in her arms. My dad was this pillar of strength trying to hold it all together, but I could see how truly scared he was too. We finally got her to the hospital, where I remember having to stay alone in the waiting room with my other sister, holding her tight as we both cried. We had no idea if our sister was even okay. There were some nice nurses and administrators that sat with us and tried to keep us calm. But it wasn't until we saw our parents and heard everything was okay that we could breathe a sigh of relief.

It had to be the longest night of our entire lives. Thankfully, my sister was fine. They broke her fever and she was allowed to go home with us that night. But it didn't stop us from worrying if it would happen again.

Jennifer Watson

Luckily, our grandparents had their summer camp trailer in Pennsylvania, not too far from where we were, so we went and stayed with them for a few days. As a mother who witnessed her own baby take a seizure once, I can understand now why we would go there instead of straight home. My poor mother (and father) were so scared about it happening again, that they needed the security of my grandparents until we all felt better that she wouldn't have another seizure. None of us could relax and enjoy ourselves. But what we did do was come together even closer as a family, and realize how much we loved each other.

For me, I could have lost my sister. Flashing through my young brain was how mean I was to her sometimes, or how I would refuse to play with her because she was an "annoying little sister." There is something about seeing your sister's eyes roll to the back of her head and then her body go lifeless that makes you realize, it's not that important if she wants to play with your favorite Barbie doll—what's important is that she is alive to play with it. A sister is a gift—two of them is a blessing. And I am so grateful everything turned out just fine that night.

5. Cousin Love: Navigating Puberty in New Jersey

Growing up the eldest of all my siblings and cousins at home was tough at times. The age gap between me and my younger sister was 5 years, and all other children were born after her. Always too old to fit in with the other kids, but not quite old enough to be with the adults, I found it much easier to retreat to my room to be myself; I fit in there.

So whenever we would visit (or be visited by) two of my older girl cousins from out-of-state, I was ecstatic. I absolutely adored them. They would treat me just like another sister, and doted on me. One trip in particular stood out when we visited them in New Jersey. I was a tween, but without much guidance. I didn't know what questions to ask my mom, otherwise I know she would have told me about all the different things I needed to know growing up. My cousins took that role on, and helped me to mature in many ways.

It sounds silly, but they taught me the most basic girly things that profoundly changed my life. Things I just didn't know how to do on my own and was ashamed to ask anyone about. I learned all about washing my hair and not being afraid of the water coming down on my head. They also taught me the right way to shave so I wouldn't cut myself. A little unconventional learning all of this from my cousins, but it did the trick, and I certainly felt like a "big girl." Afterwards, they made me feel like a princess as they played dress up with my hair, teaching me how to style it in different ways.

Butterfly Travels

I remember learning how to do a French braid, and they graciously allowed me to practice on them. (They were really good sports in between "ows".) They also showed me how to put on makeup, and even though at the time I was not allowed yet to wear it to school, knowing the basics was helpful for when I finally was old enough.

We would then dress up and pretend we were rockstars, and I really felt comfortable with my own imagination around them. They put on the radio and we would belt out the most popular songs, signing Debbie Gibson into our hairbrush microphones, and making up dances. They never made me feel judged, and they opened me up to having fun. There were bunkbeds there, so we had a big ole girly sleepover party and I got to sleep on the top bunk and tell stories and giggle all night. I was so used to keeping all of this creative, playful energy locked up inside—even with my friends back home, I didn't feel a level of security where I can just let myself be the crazy me that I was inside. Here, with my cousins, I was safe.

They also taught me courage on this particular trip. I had been unsuccessful in learning how to ride a bike without training wheels, and had given up on myself. I felt like my dad did, too. I just wasn't athletic or very coordinated, and my fears about failing (him and myself) stopped me from asking to try again. And it was never pushed on me, so I wasn't forced to face my fear. I thought I would never learn and tried to pretend it didn't bother me, or that I "hated bike-riding" and just didn't want to do it, but watching my friends back home riding bikes made me really sad. Why couldn't I just get it like everyone else?

So when my cousins asked me to go for a bike ride, I shamefully told them I didn't know how. Instead of just saying okay, we will do something else, my oldest cousin turned around and said, "Well, today is the day you are going to learn." So she took me out

> *I felt a sense of freedom and acceptance for who I was.*

and gave me some serious tough love. I fell, and was told to get over it and get back on it. There was no mercy—she even copped to making fun of me for being such a cry-baby until I found the strength within to try again and again until I got it right. And guess what—I did. I finally learned to ride a bike, and I did it on a rocky, hilly, uphill dirt road. I was pretty damn proud of myself.

As a reward for learning how to ride a bike, my uncle said he wanted to take me on a "real" bike. With my mom's heart in her throat (and my father's encouraging "let her be"), I hopped onto a motorcycle with my uncle and drove through the local streets. I've never been on a motorcycle since, but I remember the exhilaration of the wind in my hair, the freedom of driving so fast and the sense of accomplishment from overcoming my fears of failure. It was the perfect reward.

What a lesson in growing up that trip had been for me. It was so incredibly nice to have someone closer to my age to hang out with who understood me—and who I could ask for advice, and talk about those things I was still naïve about but curious to learn. I felt a sense of freedom and acceptance for who I was, and enjoyed exploring all of the things a young girl should explore. My cousins helped ease me into pre-adulthood with kindness, wisdom and non-judgment. And I am so grateful for their profound role in helping me to navigate these very scary, uncharted waters of womanhood.

6. Over (and Into) the Frost Valley River

I think the first time I truly realized I was an outcast was during my 9th grade field trip. It was my first time away from home without my family, and the anxiety had already set in. You know how it feels to be picked last for the team? Well, that rarely bothered me, because I "knew" it had nothing to do with me and everything to do with my lack of athletic ability.

Until this trip. On the trip to Frost Valley, we got to stay in little houses in groups of four. Prior to the trip, we had the opportunity to sign up to stay with who we wanted. None of my so-called friends approached me to stay with them, and when I looked at the sign-up sheets, they were all in full houses. There was not one person, with an opening, who wanted me with them. I was heartbroken.

Do you know what house WAS open though? The one with the "outcasts": a girl who was made fun of for never talking; a girl who got made fun of for smelling like pea soup; and a girl who was made fun of for being just plain weird. And then there was me. To this day, I am grateful not to know the actual words used to make fun of me, though I could just imagine between my weight, glasses and retainer, it was not flattering.

I was mortified. Now me, I had always been kind to these girls. Yet I will admit, to save myself from being the target, I would laugh along whenever they were made fun of. But to their faces,

I always felt bad and just couldn't find it in me to be cruel. But I certainly could find it in me to be judgmental. I was in a house with the school outcasts, and I just didn't know how to show my face. I didn't know how I was going to go on this trip and enjoy myself.

It wasn't an easy trip, and it certainly wasn't my best. I found some humor in it though along the way. When we got to the cabin, the bathrooms were filthy. Trained by a wonderfully clean mother, and my Virgo instincts, I had Lysol with me and made sure that our bathroom sparkled before we could even use it. My "friends" had made fun of me for bringing Lysol with me, but my roommates certainly were appreciative. I know it sounds odd, but it was my way of showing I cared about us all, and that I wanted to be a good roomie.

And I was—and so were they. I was surprised at how much fun I had with our late night chats, getting to know them and just laughing about the silliest things. And when it came time to merge with the rest of our class, they always allowed me to join them so I didn't feel alone. It was kind of them, and it helped to be wanted by someone. But this was 9th grade, and it was hard to live with the sting of being ignored and laughed at by people who you thought to be your friends, and watching them all have fun, and not inviting you. I mean, sure, there was a limit of 4 people per cabin; but was there also a limit on how many people can hang out together? Clearly, there was. I just couldn't understand why I was so ostracized.

So throughout the whole trip, I felt like a loner. I kept to myself, and listened to the all of the teacher presentations, appreciated the nature around me and looked for ways to have a little fun. I tried to keep my pride in tact and not let anyone see me cry, or know how hurt I was on the inside. But that didn't fare too well. You see, I also

> *I tried to keep my pride in tact and not let anyone see me cry, or know how hurt I was on the inside.*

had another problem—wherever I went, accidents happened. At birthday parties, I would accidentally break something; or get kicked in the face by a cartwheel and have to go to the emergency room for stitches. You know, awesomely awkward stuff.

So my experience at Frost Valley was no different. We were hiking along a waterway, which I can't recall the name of, but whose name I remember reflected its dangerousness. It was extremely rocky, with rapid water rushing through it, which led to a deadly drop. We had stopped to take a look at the water, and I, like many other kids, stepped onto a rock nearby to get a better look. Now, I was on a completely dry rock, I wasn't monkeying around like the others, or peering too far over, but somehow I ended up in the water. I can remember the water rushing at me as I grabbed onto a large rock. Luckily, a boy from my class was right by me and saw me fall in, and helped me out. He got me to calm down, reached out his hand and then pulled me out. Had it not been for this boy, and his quick actions, I do not know if I would be alive to talk about it today.

Oh, did I mention that this particular boy happened to be my longtime middle school crush? So along with gratitude was an even deeper sense of mortification. Luckily, even in his teasing of me afterwards, he was never cruel about it, and kept checking in to see if I was okay. His kindness helped me get through the rest of the torment of others making fun of me. I have never been suicidal in my entire life, but I will admit that even then, in that moment, part of me wished he just let me be.

My friendships were never the same anymore after that trip. Pathetically, I tried and tried through the rest of my years to win over their approval. At times, I had it. At times, I was invisible again. I fit in much better with the students a year ahead of me, and they became the friends I hung out with. The others were just my classmates now—though I never understood what was so wrong with me that I was not good enough. Turns out, I may have been too good.

Who knows? I have long since lost touch with all of them, though for many of us, most high school friendships are just a part of the growing up process and don't last much longer than graduation. They serve their purpose of shared childhoods, growing pains, hurts and cherished memories, all meant to help shape our social skills for forging stronger relationships in the future. And we are always for the better because of them.

But this trip taught me something I believe my "friends" weren't ready for: the ability to see beyond a person's outside and treasure who they were on the inside. I opened my heart and mind to these "misfits"—these kindred spirits who knew the receiving end of mean laughter—and what beautiful people they were. It bonded us for the rest of our years in high school, though we never did forge friendships where we hung out. But we did have an appreciation for each other, and an unspoken code of having each other's backs. I always made time to smile, say hello and sit near them in class whenever I had the opportunity…and they reciprocated. After all, they got to know me—the fourth outcast—better as well. Because in the end, I realized I was no "better" nor "worse" than them (or my "friends"), and we were all in this together.

7. Lake Adventure: Treasured Summers

After my grandparents had gotten a summer home in a community called Lake Adventure in Pennsylvania, I looked forward to my trips there each year. I always thought it was so cool they had another "home" for the summer, and plenty of room for us to visit. I remember feeling so rustic when I was there. We would sleep all together in little bunk beds. (How fun being the oldest where I always got the top!) I can remember walking into the trailer, and to the right were two small rooms, both with a set of bunk beds each in them. Of course, I was spoiled and insisted on having the one room to myself and my sisters having the other—but since neither one of them were comfortable in the other top bunk, I was forced to share. But at least I got to stay up later than them, so that made up for it. I was such a brat at times.

My parents stayed on the pullout couch (which always fascinated me how it doubled as a kitchen table and chairs, too). Then there was the little kitchen, which somehow was always stocked with our favorite foods. Then the bathroom, and on the other side of that, my grandparent's "master bedroom." It was very small, but very cozy. None of us seemed to mind the close quarters, because we were all together.

I loved how at night, our family would gather together outside. We would have delicious barbecues, eating in a tent under the stars, roasting marshmallows on skewers. There was no television (and of course, no cell phones and computers), and for some reason, I always did love when that stuff wasn't around and we sat around as a family. All night we would all tell stories, hearing about my grandparent's childhoods, or adventures my parents would go on, or even things we did as babies. This was the kind of history that fascinated me—knowing where my family came from and what they were like growing up. I can still remember the teasing and joking and boisterous laughter back and forth between all of the adults. There was so much joy and love on these trips.

I remember looking forward to seeing the community events calendar as soon as we got there to see what kind of activities were going on. Although the pool was always open, I wasn't one for swimming. (Translation: I never learned how, and was too scared of drowning to be taught.) Instead, I liked checking out what the Rec Hall was doing, from playing bingo and making arts and crafts to movie time and nature walks. I loved playing bingo with my Nanny and trying to win more "money" than her. Oh, and the ice cream socials that they would have, where we got to make our own ice cream and then talk with other kids, were also a highlight.

But the best adventures were the ones I got to take myself; where I was allowed to venture out on my own within the park, and travel my own trails. I would walk down to the water, or take a new way to the Rec Hall, and come back around to my grandparent's trailer from behind. I don't think I ever took the same path twice, because I was always curious as to where one path would lead me. It was so freeing—and I would just let my imagination run wild as I was on my own. There was definitely singing and skipping when no one was looking. It was a place to let out my inner performer.

But I think part of the fun was actually the trip there. I knew we were close when the roads became empty, and we had to slow down as we passed the deer on the side of the road. And about 10 minutes before we were at the entrance, there was this little deli that we went in to get sandwiches to bring for lunch. They had the best tuna fish ever—and I think my silliest yet fondest memory of these adventures was the fight my Poppy and I used to have over who would get the end of the bread with the last of the tuna fish. (To date, I have never had a better tuna fish sandwich.) Ah, these special little family connections make the best memories.

We only were able to spend a few summers there before my grandfather got sick, and it became difficult for my grandparents to travel back there. But for the few summers I was there, I relished every moment. My cousins had since moved close by, so I also had the added enjoyment of getting to see them and be the little sister again. It was a place I treasured so much that it set the foundation for what I thought was a love of the state of Pennsylvania—where I went to college, and ultimately moved for two years. Little did I know it was not about the place, but about the people, who made it touch my heart so profoundly.

8. Toronto Tunes: A Soulmate Connection

So, fast forward two years after my Frost Valley disaster—another school trip, and another bout of anxiety before going on it. Dag nabbit, we had to choose roommates again before the trip. But this time, I did so with ease. This time, it wasn't just my grade: it was the grade ahead of me, and the grade behind me, both of which I felt more kindred connections with than my own age. And of course, by this time in my life, I felt more connections to the boys, which was pretty fun. (They happened to deal in a lot less drama.)

I don't know what was different about this trip, but I was full of self-confidence, and didn't feel so insecure. Maybe it was because I already faced the worst case scenario as an outcast and survived. Or maybe it was because I was surrounded by my fellow band members and some chorus friends—those with whom I shared a love of music.

It was the annual music competition, where we participated in a concert with other bands, choruses and orchestras around the country. This particular year, we had the opportunity to go to Toronto, and I was super excited. Road trip!!

The whole ambiance of this journey was different than any others I had been on. Something was in the air. There was definitely a sense of playfulness and adventure—and for the first time ever around other kids my age, I just let myself go be me. I let the cameras fly without being shy or worried about how I would look

> *I could be fun and just have a good time without worrying what people thought of me.*

after the pictures were developed. (Plus, there was no insta-facebook back in "those days" to worry about—you actually had to bring in your photos or an album for people to see them).

I goofed around and flirted with the boys (and it probably helped that my self-esteem was recently boosted with a switchover from glasses to contacts and a natural body shift from pubescent awkwardness to ladylike curves without the baby fat). I also was silly with all the girls, pranking our friends in other rooms, and just doing the stupid things that teenage girls did when they had "freedom." It really was a fun experience.

Especially because this wasn't all work. Sure, we had to practice and perform, but one of the days we were there we got to let loose at an amusement park. Aside from the thrill of all the rides, we got crazy with costumed characters who walked around the park, and got sick on the most amazing fruit and powdered-sugar topped funnel cake I had ever had in my entire life. (I mean, it had whipped cream, too!) Now, before you all go thinking I am some sort of real crazy for remembering something like that—remember, I do have photos of all my adventures that help trigger these awesome memories. And yes, that funnel cake was so fabulous, that I took a picture of it.

So this trip, I learned freedom. I didn't need to feel self-conscious. I could be fun and just have a good time without worrying what people thought of me—not even those I usually felt I needed approval from. I got teased for being a ditz, but this time, instead of being a target of ridicule, the teasing was affectionate. I'd laugh back with them about it, and tease them too, and we'd end up hugging. I even ended up hanging out with some of the most popular kids from school on that trip, and realized that my previously-self-declared status of being an outcast was actually unique.

I came to the realization on this trip that I am actually friendly with every type of clique imaginable in high school: the nerds (I was one of them, hidden behind my cleverly-disguised "omg I am so blonde" routine); the popular kids (who always told me I was so sweet); the music geeks (again, because we got each other), the outcasts (who continued to always have each other's backs) and even the athletes (how could you not love a girl who handed out post-game Milky Ways to the entire team?). Ha! I guess you can say I am the entire *Breakfast Club* rolled up into one—except for the "bad boy" of course. Out of all of the cliques in high school, I only had some issues with the school "dirtbags"—half judgment on my part, admittedly, and half because they knew I wasn't cool enough to come to that particular dark side.

So that awareness set me free to just be myself. And in the end, the universe rewarded me with a meeting of a boy with the most beautiful blue eyes I had ever seen. It was an instant connection— what I would learn much later in life to be my first intense soulmate encounter. (Aside: My personal belief is that we cross paths with many kinds of soulmates throughout our lives, both romantic and platonic.)

I had felt connected to people my whole life, but this was an instantaneous "I know you" type of vibe. We hit it off so well when we met, that we ended up sitting together for the bus ride home, talking forever and laughing, as if we knew each other our whole lives. It was so natural, that when I ended up falling asleep, my head ended up on his shoulder. I jerked up to feel him put my head right back down to let me know it was okay to get comfortable with him. And it wasn't this romantic, we're going to hook up kind of vibe. It was a very sweet, very affectionate, gentle vibe between us. Of course, between his eyes and his sweetness, it was all downhill for me—I developed a hardcore crush that lasted my entire senior year. But in that very moment, I felt a true, instant, effortless bond with another person—a male—and I felt safe.

I didn't know what was to lie ahead for us from there, but that trip truly opened me up to self-acceptance, and the power of what can come into your life when you surrender and just be who you are, without the mask. Consciously, I didn't have that awareness; but that first soul connection reawakened the sleeping spirit within me that remembered the softness of my soul without ego, and the journey to deeper connections had begun.

9. Great Adventure and My First Kiss

Before you get all excited about the title, thinking this is going to be a juicy romance novel-like chapter, let me set the stage for you:

My best friends were about to graduate high school, as they were a year ahead of me. I watched them all throughout the year enjoy milestones without me: a senior trip, going to the prom with their boyfriends, senioritis (bouts of not showing up to school, for those of you unfamiliar with the term). I felt the distance already forming as they were getting ready for a big transition in their lives, and I wasn't any part of it.

Don't get me wrong. My heart was so happy for them, and it was exciting to watch knowing this was about to be my journey next year. But I would be lying if I said I didn't feel the premature pangs of loneliness, or doubt that I would have as great a senior year as they all did. So when they asked me to come along on their own end-of-the-year senior trip to Great Adventure, I was thrilled to be a part of such a bittersweet memory.

I love amusements parks. I love thrill rides—the feeling of no control, being twisted and turned loop-de-loop, upside down, throwing my hands in the air as I feel the wind rush past my entire body. I even love the sappy little carousel rides, because it brings out the inner child in me. So it was a playful day, walking around the park with my dearest of friends, and their friends. We had all chipped in for a rented bus to take us to the New

Jersey park, and it was packed out with some pretty loud high schoolers.

Not everyone was from our high school though. My closest friends had brought their boyfriends (who brought their friends) from other school districts, so I was the "wheel" (or "cling-a-long" as I was affectionately called) as these couples walked through the park. It sucked at times, but thankfully, my friends would switch off going on rides with their beaus so I wasn't always a single rider. But then we caught up with another group and starting walking around with them, and there was a mix of girls and guys, not all partnered up, so I would rotate going on rides with different people, and that felt much more comfortable.

So towards the end of the night, there were these two guys who were hanging out with us, one of which was very nice to me. We would talk and laugh, and go on rides, and I thought nothing of it. Why would I? I was always the one with the crush, and not vice versa.

So imagine my surprise when my BFF asked me what I thought of him, only to reveal that he liked me. Well that sent unknown feelings through me that I've never experienced before: to be on the receiving end. (After all, nothing had ever happened romantically with my Toronto crush, so I was in very much uncharted territory.) He was a bit older than us, but only by a few years. Being armed with this knowledge made me nervous for the rest of the night, like my every move was being watched. (Oh, you think by him? No—by every one of my girlfriends, curious over what could be my life-changing moment.)

These same girls had not so subtly orchestrated a change in seating so that me and this boy just so happened to now be sitting together for the two hour bus ride home that night. Awkward,

> *Well, that unleashed 17 years of untapped love.*

indeed. We talked for a little bit, yet the shyness within me would not cease. I felt like I wanted to throw up — either because I would be disappointed if he didn't want to kiss me, or that I would disappoint him by sucking at kissing.

I had convinced myself he looked like Richard Marx (who I had a major crush on as a teenager), so that made it tougher to be cool. There was finally this moment where we were just looking at each other and smiled. I immediately looked down, and he asked if something was wrong. I couldn't speak, so he filled the void by telling me he thought I was really pretty and that he wanted to kiss me, and asked me if I wanted to kiss him.

Such an inexperienced little girl, I started laughing. Complete and utter nervous laughter, squeaking out a "maybe" and then looking back down again. Poor guy couldn't bolt because he had the window seat; so instead, he took a piece of my hair and pushed it back behind my ear, lifted my chin up and gently kissed my lips. He pulled away and looked into my eyes until I had the courage to kiss him back. Well, that unleashed 17 years of untapped love, ending up in an hour-long makeout session, followed by more innocent shoulder snuggling as we slept the rest of the trip home holding hands. (You know, I now realize that bus rides seem to be pretty lucky for me, and I should take them more often!)

After that trip, I was teased for quite a few weeks by my friends, who thanked me for the entertainment and hounded me with the endless questions about the experience, if we were now dating, do we talk, etc. Nothing did ever come from it — we talked on the phone a few times, but that was it. I didn't really feel much of a connection; either that, or I was scared shitless to actually have a boyfriend—or worse, my heart was still drawn to Toronto-boy and I couldn't move on. Ironically, a few years later when I was dating my soon-to-be husband, I ran into him and his friend at a local diner. They actually all knew each other—and of course, didn't like each other. He no longer looked like Richard Marx to me; but he still had the kindness of being the man who knew how to ease a girl into her first kiss.

10. Virginia & All that Jazz: Confessions of a Teenage Heartbreak

I came to love my band camp trips each year, traveling to different places with kindred souls who loved music—and loved being goofy and unique even more. This time, we were headed to Virginia, and as seniors, we ruled the bus. Plus, I felt like I finally had groups to fit in with somewhat, so choosing a room wasn't all that difficult, and the bus ride there was fun. This was going to be just like last year, or even better—or so I expected.

This trip was topping off what had been a whirlwind year for my heart. I was deeply crushing on my blue-eyed Toronto-boy, who had recently broken up with his third girlfriend of the year. I really adored him, and he was always sweet and helpful, but he never saw me or treated me as anything other than a friend. And it was so frustrating for me, because we could talk about anything, and we were flirtatious and playful, and everything I thought a relationship would be like. But he never made a move our entire senior year.

I thought this trip would change things. I mean, when I met him last year on our Toronto trip and had such an amazing ride home with him, I thought we would be able to rekindle that initial connection and finally make something happen. (When I love, I love loyally and for a long time, with the patience of a saint as if they will come around one day like magic. Perhaps that is a bit stalkerish; but I like to think of it as committed *LOL*)

Anyway, this trip wasn't anything like I had hoped it would be. I thought I could recreate the same kind of fun as last year—and in some ways, I did—but in many other ways, the same fire wasn't there in Virginia as it was in Toronto. And I just don't mean with my boy, but with the people I was with, too. I mostly walked along with the drama club people, since I really, really admired them—and of course, secretly wanted to be them. They were carefree, fun, silly, sing-songy, not caring what others thought of them as they were just themselves. And although they are sweet and accepting of everybody, there was still that twinge that I just didn't quite fit in. I was from jazz band; they were more chorus-driven. Funny how the difference in how you explored music also created different cliques of people and how they interacted.

I did like my jazz band people, of course, and hung out with them, too. My crush was part of jazz band, as was our friend and his girlfriend that we hung out with and were planning on going to the prom with. But for some reason, our foursome didn't really stick together during the trip until the bus ride home, so I found myself a floater again: no "home" of friends to experience this trip with. Not even with the girls I stayed with—a combo of orchestra girls (yet another different kind of group!) and some other jazz band girls with whom I didn't really feel a connection. It felt all so forced; everywhere I turned, all of the different groups had "inside jokes" that I had no inside information on, and couldn't relate to.

This was to be a common theme in my life. Likable, but just not meant to fit in with the mainstream crowd. Today, I am cool with it, but as a teenager, it's all your heart wants: to be liked by everyone and be like everyone else. I don't know why I couldn't bring myself to have the same carefree attitude as I did last time, honoring the authentic me instead of trying so hard to fit in. But I can tell you that my change in attitude definitely impacted the experience I had this time, and my sense of self-esteem and acceptance. I mean, it certainly wasn't as bad as my Frost Valley trip; but add in the disappointment of a crush barely acknowledging you, and we're talking teenage tragedy.

My crush and I talked by the end of the trip and cleared things up: it just wasn't the clarity I was expecting. He just wanted space to be with his friends—and to be free to explore certain activities I wasn't exactly on board with. But I wanted to help him. He was my friend, I cared about him and I thought he was going down a "bad" path.

Enter my very first desire to "save" someone from themselves, from their "self-destruction" (as I saw it). And every moment after that—save for a few special memories over the summer—our friendship was tarnished with my incessant savior attitude as he continued a downward spiral that was his lesson to learn. It would take me a great many years to realize what a damaging part of myself—and damaging vibration of attraction to draw in—in many, many of my relationships to come. I never was able to save him, or our friendship. Luckily, years down the road, we briefly reconnected for closure, and I got to see him as the loving, respectable family man I knew he was meant to be. It just wasn't my job to lead him there—it was his.

11. The Winds of College: From Hershey to Lancaster

Nothing can prepare you properly for college (or "real life" afterwards, or marriage, or parenthood, and so on). What a culture shock it is to remove yourself from living under the rules of your parents, with their guidance and protection, and then venture out on your own to discover yourself and your life. How exhilarating and scary all at the same time.

The college I went to was strategically placed between Hershey and Lancaster, and depending on which way the wind blew, you either had the delectable scents of the chocolate factory stimulating your olfactory senses, or the barf-inducing smell of nearby cows. It was quite an interesting place, and not at all what I expected. I based my expectations on my experience at my grandparent's place in the Poconos, not realizing that this was no vacation I was about to take. Shit was about to get real.

But not in necessarily a bad way. In an empowering way— sometimes through exciting new adventures, and other times through tough life lessons and social challenges. I had a rough first year. What started out as a great journey soon turned into a repeat of past hurts. I wasn't one to make friends easily; I am actually quite shy and it takes me a while to warm up, so I definitely had anxiety about meeting new people. But luckily, my college experience began with a trip to Jersey City with girls I met earlier in the summer at orientation, and we had such a blast. My college roommate turned out to be from a neighboring district from where I grew up, so I felt connected to her knowing that we had that location bond. And there were many wonderful girls in my all-girl dorm that were all kind and welcoming—they were terrified themselves, and we were all in the same boat together.

But soon thereafter, when I thought I had a set of friends that would be my college-lifers, my social life got turned upside down. One of my friends turned on me, and actually told me to get my own set of friends and to stop hanging out with hers. There was one friend in particular she had that I wasn't quite a fan of, who would come in my room and be extremely mean to me. In fairness, she was mean to everyone, but she certainly loved taking the most potshots at me. I was broken-hearted, and alone. Who would I eat with? Who would I go to parties with? Who would I talk to when I was having a hard time—about this?

But true to nature, I had made good friendships with individual girls here and there. (I just really am not a group person; I am much better with one-on-one friendships.) Luckily, this opened up some doors for me to find my own crew. Actually, a few different ones, which was authentically more of my style. Again, I found myself admiring those in the music and drama concentrations, feeling completely accepted as I truly was. And then there was the group of friends I forged the strongest alliance with; who I ended up sharing a living space with, and who were there to welcome me back with love after my 6-month departure to Spain.

Even within my circle of friends, there were, of course, fights and struggles and hurts, but for the most part, I made friends with the most amazing people who I am still connected to today. You don't go through an experience like college without making strong bonds that last a lifetime; we literally grew up into adults together. We created amazing memories together. We made bad, life-lesson decisions together. We made mistakes and laughed about them

> *I based my expectations on my experience in the Poconos, not realizing this was no vacation I was about to take. Shit was about to get real.*

(like thinking a free hair modeling gig would be a good idea; yeah, not so much). We supported each other (oftentimes with pints of Ben and Jerry's in the hallways). We cried when one of us was heartbroken and hurt. We learned from each other. We opened our eyes to each other's perfections and our flaws, and we loved each other for them. Peace was even restored between my former friend and I, as we navigated through our lives. And to this day, I am grateful for the friendships this 4-year adventure brought into my life.

There was so much that I learned from this particular journey. I learned how to become an adult and take care of myself. I learned to rely on myself, and both support and get support from others when I needed to. I tested my own moral and value system and survived. I learned how childish I could really be—both as in playfulness, and as in cattiness towards others. I developed new tastes and was introduced to new perspectives and new ways of life. I explored my creative side, and changed majors a few times trying to figure out what I really wanted to be when I grew up.

I worked cameras behind the scenes on the college tv station. I started as a sundae bar girl and graduated into a student manager of the café. I tutored others in writing and landed an internship in marketing at a senior community center. I played on the swings at the neighborhood "Fort," enjoyed fishbowl Hurricane drinks underage at the local bars, played Truth or Dare, sang into hairbrushes and danced my butt off at our weekend dances. I survived on ramen noodle soup and mac and cheese at times, learned how to avoid the cold rush of water in the shower after a community flush, and along with my roomie, invited strange boys from another college to come visit us after meeting them online.

Maybe some of these seem so mild or silly to you, but each of us has our own adventure that we go on, and the moments that mean the most to us. For me, it was the little silly things that I remember. I will never forget the profound moments either, but those are easy to see how they change your life. But what really helps to build your character, your spirit and your experience are those things that are uniquely influential to you. And for me, it was all of these different ways of expanding myself outside of a very contained box that helped me to open up my mind and heart to all the possibilities that were to lie ahead for me.

12. Falling for Fell's Point, Baltimore

College is where my real adventures began. Up until that point, I had just been to a few local places, mostly just school trips and an occasional family vacation—and not that I wasn't grateful for those experiences, it's just that going to college opened up my freedom to explore on my own.

I had the chance to travel with my roomies wherever I wanted to go, whenever I wanted to go. A trip to Jersey City; spring break in Ocean City; going to my friend's house in Philly; tours of local Lancaster, Hershey and Harrisburg; and of course, those oh so fun road trips home playing *New York State of Mind* by Billy Joel as we crossed over the Verazzano Bridge.

But the trips I remember most fondly are the ones to Baltimore, Maryland. From the very first moment I entered Baltimore, I fell in love. I don't know what it was about the place, but I wanted to live there one day. I had friends from home who went to college there; friends from my college who lived there; family there—it was a whole different world for me, but not quite sure why. It was just a plain old city, and had the same old suburbs like I had experienced elsewhere. But there was a kind of magic in the air that kept drawing me back there, over and over. I kept finding reasons to visit Baltimore throughout college—and even years later after graduation and marriage.

Butterfly Travels

One of my strongest memories was a time I was visiting a friend at Towson—and if I remember correctly, it was my first trip there. We drove down there and stayed with her and her roommates, and we went out to this strip of bars at Fell's Point.

This was a big deal for me. I had been to underage-approved clubs and managed to sneak into a bar, but at (my) naive age of 19, I never experienced bar hopping—or using a "fake" ID to get in. A girl I knew back home had given me her old license—she was maybe 7 years older than I was, but we were uncannily familiar in appearance. I remember being so nervous about getting caught and going to jail (my imagination might be a little extreme), and my friend did everything she could to calm me down so that it wasn't obvious to the bouncers. I mean, I have a transparent face—I can't lie or hide the truth for shit. It is impossible for me.

So we get up to the bouncers and hand them our IDs. He takes one look at mine, and lets me in. Ironically—my girlfriend did not get in; the kicker being, she actually WAS 21, but they didn't believe her license was really hers. Eventually they let her in, but it was pretty funny that I stressed and got in no problem, and she had the issue.

So we all get in, and I am in awe. Yup—in awe of an overcrowded, sticky-floored, loud, obnoxious dance club. The music was pumping and I could get any drink I wanted. It was such an amazing feeling to have this freedom, and for the first time ever, I had no inhibitions. I wasn't afraid of dancing, or what I looked like, or if guys would be interested. I was just loving every part of my new environment—and with my guard down, that's probably why I had such a blast. We danced all night. I met a guy, danced with him and even kissed him on the dance floor. It was pretty hot for my first real club experience. I felt on top of the world, and I actually had very little alcohol in me. I was much more high on life experience than anything else.

So we jumped from bar to club and back, and with my newfound confidence, I didn't sweat the fake ID. No other place was as "magical" as the first one we were at, but we all ended up having a blast before taking a taxi back home in the wee hours of the morning, as we sang Green Day at the top of our lungs.

The next day, we went on to enjoy the sights of the Inner Harbor—and I loved it there, between the water and the energy. So with the fun nightlife and the calm day place, it was easy for me to just want to move my whole life there. I ended up going back several times—enjoying it every time, in different ways. At the time, I was single with no specific plans for life after graduation, so I had decided that when I did graduate, I would be moving to Baltimore and would find a job there. It was my heart, my passion, my future.

Little did I know that all my plans were about to change because of a boy.

13. An Introduction to Fame: The Philly Arena

It wasn't until my second semester of sophomore year in college that I finally got what I always wanted: a boyfriend. My whole life was turned upside down, and would never be the same. I even knew back then—the very moment that I met him—that he would end up being my husband. He was unexpected; something I desired, but never imagined would throw a monkey wrench into my life plan. I was going to be a businesswoman—a successful executive who traveled the world; marriage and maybe kids was something I would think about later in my 20s, if I got around to it.

But all that changed when I met him. And he wasn't the type of guy you would expect a straight-A "golden girl" who was nauseatingly well-behaved to end up with. Not the doctor or lawyer my parents had banked on for me. Oh no—apparently I had as much yearning for adventure in relationships as I did in my travels: I found me a professional wrestler.

Oh, it shocked me at first, too. When I met him and he talked about being a wrestler, I assumed he meant college wrestling on a mat. I soon came to realize that he meant television, in-the-ring wrestling. Say what? I had no idea what kind of adventure I was really about to go on. Unbeknownst to me at the time, it actually activated a very crucial part of my soul that had been locked up since birth.

> *I was in my own kind of spotlight, with fans instantly curious about me as if I was a first lady celebrity myself.*

Enter my first experience at his wrestling arena in Philadelphia. The spotlights on the ring. The being escorted through the locker room to meet the "boys" (many of whom were extremely famous wrestlers). Seeing all of the behind-the-scenes action. Watching my man enter the ring like a rockstar as fans chanted his name and cheered. But for me, what shocked me most was how much I loved being "his" girl, with everyone wondering who I was. I was in my own kind of spotlight, with fans instantly curious about me and associating with me as if I was a first lady celebrity myself. I gotta say, that kind of attention was extremely intoxicating.

But my adventures as his girl were not always so amazing. In fact, many were downright horrifying. My very first trip with him to the arena, I sat in horror alongside strangers in the audience as I watched the leg of a chair go through his chin and blood spurt out all over the ring. I knew no one there, and I had to wait patiently in the arena, without any communication about how he was doing, while he was rushed to the hospital for stitches. Suddenly, what happened to be a very cool profession turned awfully real and terribly frightening. What the hell was this guy into? But by this time, I had already developed feelings for him, and for me, there was no turning back. I was with him all the way.

For every ladder match. Every beating of the Singapore cane that left him with bruises all over his back. Every cut to the forehead to make it bloody for an exciting match. Every kiss of another woman I had to stomach because it was part of the storyline. Every new ring partner he had, and his innovation to take things to the next level, from barbed wire matches to playing with fire.

Every fake "friend" I had to put up with because he needed them for a ride somewhere. Every betrayal from these fake friends, as they only wanted to get close to me to feel closer to him. Every after party—one of which almost put my life into danger when a female fan of his (admittedly) wanted to put a roofie in my drink so that she could take advantage of me sexually. He did everything he could to protect me from all this; he really did, and it made me love him more. But eventually, I learned that the spotlight was not worth all of this. At least not this way.

Eventually, I stopped going to the shows. I stopped asking about the bruises, concussions and perverted storylines. I stopped wanting to take care of the wounds, or deal with the after-effects. I became so resentful of his profession, and how it (and my attitude towards it) was destroying our relationship, and our family— but most importantly, how I thought it was destroying him. Physically, mentally, emotionally.

The tour of the wrestling world certainly opened my eyes to a lot. I left my world of innocence and saw what "street smarts" were really all about at times. I learned that I really did love and crave that spotlight, and loved being that center of attention. But I also saw firsthand the price one pays for the spotlight. And I'm still not entirely sure what—if anything—made all of it worth it.

14. A New Home, A New Me: My Barcelona Life

If ever there was an experience that shaped and transformed my life, it was this one. Second semester junior year of college, after my one year anniversary with my boyfriend, I set out on my dream trip: a six month study abroad program in Barcelona, Spain. My whole education was set up for this moment: an experience of a lifetime. All through childhood, I had watched friends go to Europe and yearned to be like them. We never had the money to go, so even when school trip opportunities came up, I couldn't go, and it crushed me. But finally, this was my moment. This was my trip. This was my journey, and I was going it alone.

I am actually struggling to find words to describe the profoundness of this experience for me. Wow, did it pack a punch of adulthood every step of the way. Faced with old hurts of feeling left out when groups of peers and friends formed, I struggled immensely with a mean, stuck-up roommate upon arrival and had massive anxiety attacks. I will admit—I almost called it quits and went back home. I was on that very edge of failure, and I couldn't take this loneliness and rejection any longer. It hurt my heart—and affected my health. I ended up at an infirmary, scared out of my mind in a foreign country with all that I loved back home, and no one but a few kind teachers to support me. I was in over my head. What made me think that I could travel by myself to a foreign country, with no support system, no job, minimal Spanish speaking skills and no fucking clue what I was doing? I cried for nights on end. My new host parents were very kind, but pushy about me choosing to stay alone in my room instead of getting out with friends. They made me feel even worse about not having friends or anyone to hang out with. I was more alone than ever before. I didn't even have my best friend, or my boyfriend, or even my mother to talk to. Completely, and utterly, alone.

I actually cannot recall what shifted in me, or when. But one day I just seemed to have woken up, and decided to take my life into my own hands. Yup, I was alone. Hey!! I was finally ALONE! There was no greater freedom than being alone in a foreign country, and all this time I was crying about it. My whole life I had wished to be away from rules and expectations, and here I was, wasting away exactly what I wished for. And here is where my transformation began.

I no longer sat in the house. I only had class 3 times a week, all in the afternoon (sweet, I know!), so every single weekday morning, I began my routine. Having little money, I walked everywhere. I started walking an hour and half each way to the beach every morning. Port Olimpic had become my special place. I remember that walk fondly. If I went back there today, 20 years later, I could still remember the path. Up around the corner, passed my favorite café where I had hot choco-latte every morning, passed the university I attended, down the long and busy highway, passed the zoo and then onto the path to the beach.

On days I didn't have class, I extended my walk home passed my house to the Industrial Park, where I worked out in my very first gym ever, listening to mixed tapes sent to me by my loved ones. I gave up soda, which tasted horrid overseas. I ate pretty healthy, and really got in shape. I walked so much, and the little gym work helped with toning. I lost so much weight—40 pounds—and had such a dark tan (and new fashionable wardrobe) that I was literally unrecognizable by my family when I returned home.

> *It was as if this trip brought to light everything I ever wanted in life so clearly: independence, success and freedom.*

I learned how to become healthy while living in Spain, and took care of myself. I also eventually found a group of friends to hang out with, and we would cook at each other's houses, go to the bars at night, frequent our favorite pool hall weekly, go to the beach and then later party at Port Olimpic's strip of dance clubs. Eventually, life just fell into place there. I did things I never thought I would do. I mean, besides giving up soda and actually going to the gym, which was a big deal for me, considering my obsession with food.

I would walk down the street at 3am completely unafraid. Probably not the smartest thing for a young American blonde to do in Spain, but I did it, and did it often, feeling the liberation. Nothing would hurt me. I knew it in my soul. I needed to face the fear of being on my own more than the fear of any danger lurking in the shadows. It was MY shadow I had to be afraid of. The one that always held me back. That one that said, "You're not good enough. You're going to fail." Well, I shut that voice of inner nonsense down when I proved it wrong. Self-confidence was mine for the taking, and I embraced it whole-heartedly.

Along with being in a foreign country, came the enjoyment of exploring another culture. I tried new foods; learned about new traditions; became fascinated with the history of art and architecture. I learned Ethics from a really hot professor who spoke Catalan (a French/Spanish dialect of Barcelona) and survived both my (thankfully unreturned) attraction to him and the class. Not bad earning an A in a class where I had no idea what the hell the professor was saying day in and day out. I formed strong bonds with the people there, all of which I have sadly lost contact with, but who remain in my heart as my crew of transformation travelers. But what I took away most from this experience was my awareness of American judgment and superiority; of our close-mindedness (at least mine) and sense of entitlement.

Assimilating back into home/school life in America was one of the absolute hardest experiences of my entire life. I had such intolerance all of a sudden for any prejudiced remarks, even in "harmless" jokes. I felt constricted by the rules and confinements of my parents once again. I broke up with my boyfriend because I felt smothered and unsure if he was what I wanted anymore. It was as if this trip brought to light everything I wanted in life so clearly: independence, success and freedom. What I wanted more than anything in this entire world was freedom. Spain gave that to me, and America took it back.

I knew it before I left, too. I sobbed before leaving Spain, my whole body rejecting the notion of going back home—as much as I missed those I loved so dearly. I just knew what awaited me there. I was a "new" person going back to an "old" life. They say you can't go back to the past—although true, you can certainly be thrust into it without a safety net, and find yourself back under the lock and key of expectations (of others AND mine) without blinking. I have never been the same, though at this point in my life, I have never been closer to that sense of freedom. And I can feel it within my reach again.

I've come to realize that Spain was only a place, and that it wasn't about the location or the experience, but rather, the space to explore who I truly was on a deep level. It was only a mental representation of what has always been in my heart. Once I had that awareness that "Barcelona" has been inside of me all along, I discovered that to get back to that place of independence, success and freedom, all I had to do was find the Spain within again.

15. I Left My Heart in Europe

My study abroad experience encompassed 6 months of my life; I would be remiss if I did not spend at least two chapters on this. After all, my adventures took me beyond my "home" in Barcelona, and in fact, contributed to a very deep sense of awakening and independence.

As a group of study abroad students, we traveled throughout Spain, from Madrid to Granada, and a few places in between. Mostly, it was architecture, ruins and art museums, all of which were pretty interesting. One of my favorite Spanish cultural experiences was to watch an authentic flamenco dancing show. I remember being captivated by their brilliant colors and rhythmic movements. But my all-time favorite place in Spain was where I had the pleasure of living, in Barcelona. Nothing beats the culture of the people you pass on the streets, those who serve you in the cafes, and the charm of the musicians alongside the metros (subways).

Embracing the different cultures was something I truly enjoyed doing throughout my travels. I was always amazed by how each country was so different, and magical, in its own way. I had a spring break from Universidad where I had the opportunity to travel to a few different countries. As a college student, the popular thing to do was to buy a Eurorail pass and travel by train. These trains were pretty cool—and with beds perfect for traveling students, it helped us save a lot of money from staying

> *Twenty years later, I can still see, smell, hear, taste and feel very specific memories from every part of this journey.*

in hostels. Packed with little clothing, toiletries and a supply of peanut butter, jelly and crackers to supplement a student budget, off I was to explore.

I mostly traveled with a group of friends, breaking up into different pairs, or going alone at different portions of the trip, depending on our individual itineraries and interests. First up was France—and the infamous Eiffel Tower. As a girl missing her boyfriend, traveling with a guy friend she normally didn't get along with under "real life" circumstances, the much-spoken-about romance of Paris was definitely lost on me. Maybe that was it, but I wasn't too impressed with Paris. The tower was just a tall metal structure. A Café Au Lait, though beautiful to sit outside with, with a view of the Arc de Triomphe down the street, was nothing more than an overrated coffee. Even the Louvre, with its Mona Lisa and other historical paintings, did not make me fall in love with the city. I found it to be a huge disappointment; my romantic heart was a bit shattered. Perhaps one day I will go back with the right person and see it for its possibilities. C'est la vie!

Next on the list was Italy. Ahhh, now there was a country that stole my heart. We stopped off first together in Pisa, my guy friend and I parting ways, while another girlfriend of mine met back up with me to do some exploring. I have to quickly mention Pisa because although it was merely a stopover, luckily, right outside of our station was the Leaning Tower, and I got to take a picture of it. Now, back in "those days" we did not use digital cameras; we had cameras with film and we couldn't see the pictures we took until after they were developed. So, when I got home, I learned that somehow, I leaned with the Tower and straightened it. Classic moment, realizing my Leaning Tower of Pisa was not leaning because I had tilted to take it. My family had a good laugh at that.

Back to my adventures. In Italy, we visited three cities: Rome, Florence and Venice. Rome was amazing, with its cultural structures, the ruins of the Colosseum and outstanding food. Here was a place rich with history that I could appreciate. Florence was breathtaking. The whole city was made of these exquisitely colorful buildings that were so unique, and a leather street market that was to die for. Finally, I had found a marketplace that called my name…and my wallet.

Venice was also extremely interesting to travel through, as we took gondolas everywhere. We also traveled by boat to a glass-blowing factory where we learned how glass was made, and that was pretty interesting as well. I had realized that these were the kinds of experiences that really spoke to me. Yes, the historical stuff was very nice, but to really get into modern day culture, and see how people lived and worked, and the creations they made and sold, was so much more fascinating to me.

My friend and I continued on to Switzerland together. At one point in our journey, not sure exactly when, we had been on the train that passed through Austria. Neither of our passes included travel through that country, so when we came to a stop there, we were almost thrown off the train. We had no intention of going to the country, but the route we were taking was going through there. We took a chance and stayed on the train, since it was night time, we were low on funds and a little scared of what would await us with no hotel reservation in a country we weren't authorized to be in. Luckily, the conductor hadn't come through again, and the very next stop was a country and city we were planning on going to. We averted disaster, thankfully, but not without a few anxiety attacks—since neither of us were the type to take those kinds of risks or take advantage of a system.

Upon arriving in Switzerland, we immediately were goofballs and went in search of Swiss cheese and chocolate. Oh the Americans that we were, didn't realize their definitions of cheese and chocolate were completely different—but oh so much more delicious! It was one of our favorite countries. Very quaint and charming, as you could imagine. We decided to take the *Sound of Music* tour, and were surprised to learn that much of the movie was actually filmed in Switzerland, and not Austria. We walked through the gardens, gazebo and other key scenes, the two of us singing and dancing (while getting glares from the other tourists). Such a fun tour—probably the best I have been on in my entire life.

One last country I had visited was Germany, which I went to on my own. I went to Munich, thinking that I would feel so connected to my German heritage while I was there. My grandfather is 100% German, so I thought I would feel at home. But I didn't. It was beautiful and endearing, for certain. I even decided to go to the local Biergarten; how could I go to Germany and not have a beer and a hearty meal? The music was playful (as were the gentlemen hitting on me), but that was one trip where I was glad to only have chosen a day's visit, and went to bed safely tucked in early for a good night's rest.

Thus ended my adventure through Europe, collecting coins, souvenirs and my hobby of buying something in every city I went to that represented it or how I felt about it. To this day, I still have every little memento in my curio cabinet, which has since grown. All in all, my adventures were full of lessons. To not believe everything you hear. To find the golden nugget of cultural difference in every place you go. To have the courage to travel on your own, whether you know the language or not, and find your way through. To treasure every moment in your heart until you can visit again. Twenty years later, and I can still see, smell, hear, taste and feel very specific memories from every part of this journey. And as I sit here writing this and reliving it, I am overwhelmed with the remembrance of joy and happiness.

Oh—one more place. On our flight back home, we had a stopover in Amsterdam. I grabbed a coaster from the airport, and called it a visit. Or maybe it was just a placeholder for when I returned to Europe for another tour. I have yet to get back there (at least, to this area), but I have a dream of bringing my children back to see where I had lived, to some of my favorite places, and explore new ones, such as Greece and Austria. The door to my now internationally inquisitive heart had undoubtedly been opened.

16. A London Proposal

It would be a few years until I was able to return to Europe. And I remember what a challenge it was to get there. Before even getting to London, my boyfriend and I had taken an overnight trip to Williamsburg—a trip that was not sanctioned by my mom, which ended up in a horrific fight between us. She had said that while I was in college, she couldn't stop me from traveling with him to go wrestling, but since it was the summer and I was under her roof (even after my six months living by myself in Europe), I still had to live by her rules. Although now I can appreciate the discipline and love behind providing me with a sound moral structure, my "worldly" 20-something attitude didn't.

No worries—everything with my mom ended up just fine and we hugged it out. I didn't regret going though, against her wishes—my boyfriend and I ended up reconnecting, and reaffirming our relationship. For me, it actually was my pre-cursor to saying "yes" to marriage, because my hesitancy in being with him before was truly all about that fear of commitment.

So when I found out he was going to London a few months later, I was insanely jealous. London was on my wishlist, but not something I was able to get to while living in Spain. I'd watch my boyfriend travel all over, to Japan, to California, to all of these places I've never been, but when I heard London, and that it happened to be during Valentines Day week, I secretly wished and wished inside that I could go somehow. My wish came true

Butterfly Travels

when we were at a family gathering and he announced that he was taking me to London. Immediately, panic set in, and I looked at my mother—who thankfully, was smiling, as she had already given her blessing. I must have asked a thousand times if she was sure she was okay with it, and when I saw the plane ticket with my name on it, I knew it was true.

This was our first real, official adventure together. I would hear about his travels to places, and he sat and listened to mine, and for the first time, we would be able to share an experience. He had been to London before, so he knew all the right places to take me: Big Ben, Piccadilly Circus, Buckingham Palace—and we had a blast. We stayed in a suite with other wrestlers and their girlfriends, and man, was that a different kind of experience in itself.

One night, the night before Valentines Day, my boyfriend had taken me out to dinner. It was a very nice dinner, but the conversation seemed a little odd. He kept asking me about some of the men in my past, and was trying to have me compare him to them, and I just thought it was so strange. He was on edge about something, and I actually thought that now that he had me back, he was trying to pay me back and set me up for a future dumping when we got home to the States.

Turns out, it was the exact opposite. We had gone back to the hotel room after dinner to hang out, and had just gotten ready for bed, when I turned around to see him down on one knee holding a ring in his hand. It took me completely by surprise because I had told him I did not want to be proposed to on a holiday. I wanted it to be our own special day, and here it was, now Valentines Day.

He looked so nervous, and I was in a state of shock. Was this really happening? Of course I said yes, and had him put the ring

> *I learned then and there that I set my expectations too high.*

on my finger, and it was a sweet moment. He looked relieved and happy, and the ring was beautiful—exactly the very simple pear-shaped stone I asked for. The moment should have ended there, it being nice that he chose London to be the place to ask me to spend forever with him, and me shelving the disappointment of being asked in a hotel room in an unspecial way. (What? Don't judge me. That is a very important moment in a young girl's life, and when you love romance as much as I do, with a man who knows how much you love that romance, you would understand. And in about two sentences, you WILL understand. Wait for it.)

The next words out of his mouth were, "We were supposed to have dinner in a restaurant that overlooked Buckingham Palace, and I was going to ask you to be my princess forever. But reservations fell through, sorry." See there? Now that was a romantic kind of proposal, and hearing that disappointed my heart, and my mind immediately thought, *um, you could have walked me past the palace and said the same thing.*

It was one thing when I just thought he wasn't creative, or his nerves got the best of him and he was just worried about whether I would accept or not. But to go ahead and tell me about this fabulous other plan he had, and that it didn't work out, and that this was his backup plan? I know I sound ungrateful, and yes, I was. I should have loved every moment of that special time with him, and not judged it or had an inner temper tantrum. I was 22. I was a little too young to get the concept just yet.

But it was sweet, and I did accept it for what it was and showed off my ring and my new fiancé with pride. His heart was all in, and his intentions were loving, and I knew that. But remember that trip to the Eiffel Tower where I thought it missed the romance because of the company I kept? That feeling came rushing back to me in London. I learned then and there that I set my expectations too high, and that I would need to learn to live with a lack of creative romance my entire life. A small price to pay for finally having the engagement and relationship I wanted my entire life, right? At least we loved each other, and that needed to be all that mattered.

I know it sounds crazy, but a little part of my hope died that day. I never felt the sparks. I never felt the wow. There were no magical fireworks like I expected there would be when you decided to marry someone. I kinda just felt like we were both going through the motions, like this is what we had to do, and it began to sink in that this was it for us—for the both of us. This was setting the stage for the rest of our lives. And it did in a way. His good intentions never came through; something always happened to cancel, change or ruin any plans for something special. And my expectations were too high to live up to, that I guess he just stopped trying all together.

Sad how much foreshadowing there was in this one trip; in this one moment. Two lost souls with every intention of loving each other forever, but just not being the right fit. Our gut instincts were yelling at both of us, yet we were blindly ignoring them all the way. But there was a higher purpose to come from our union, and we gave it all that we had until we could give no more.

17. A Sales Girl on the Road: My Trade Show Excursions

My dream of traveling as part of my job came true when I joined a family organization during my engagement years. It was exciting for me to be chosen to go on various trips with the different bosses, or on behalf of the organization, and both strengthened my knowledge and skills while satiating my desire for adventure. Not everywhere we went was profound, but it always was interesting to see new places. I applied my approach to these new places as I did to different countries, understanding that new cities and states could be just as diverse from New York as cities throughout Europe were from each other.

Some of the places I remember included Virginia, Maine, upstate New York, Atlantic City, and random places in Pennsylvania, to name a few. Virginia was my very first experience traveling overnight with two of my bosses, and that was quite an adventure. I knew I was working for a different kind of company when we encountered some mishaps along the way, and they weren't concerned that some new girl was sitting in the backseat watching the whole thing. Yup—I was already one of the family.

I also remember my deep level of embarrassment over having to wear my really thick glasses at night in the car because my contacts needed to be disinfected for at least 6 hours, and we had to be at the trade show bright and early in just a few hours. My one boss to this day still jokes with me how he remembers my "coke bottles." It really was the beginning of a beautiful, healthy relationship with someone who has been like a brother to me—who clearly, enjoyed teasing me like one from the get go.

My adventures then branched out to traveling with a co-worker of mine, who has since left the company but is still a dear friend. I remember our first assignment was to a trade show in Maine, where we took a "puddle jumper" plane and she was petrified. Once we landed, all was well, as we stepped out into beautiful Portland, Maine. Where we stayed, the streets were these sweet little cobblestone roads. After work, we enjoyed walking through the streets, just talking, and it felt so good to be on a trip with someone I felt comfortable with, and it was like I left all my worries behind. We had a fabulous dinner, and charged wine to our expense account and had a complete blast. I had never been on a trip before like this for business, but she had, so I had followed her lead from her past experience on how to not worry about the budget. Little did we know, budget was a big deal, and we overstepped. Oops! That was a mistake we would never make again.

We were allowed to venture together again shortly after to Atlantic City for another show. My co-worker was a clever one, and since we were in Sales, and we were on a budget, she networked us into getting another company to buy us dinner and drinks, and had a blast again—but not in a way that would misrepresent our company. We always took our day work seriously, and made the leads and connections we were supposed to. But when off the clock, that was our time to enjoy the trip as we liked.

So after dinner, we did a little gambling, a little boardwalk exploring and a little dancing. Trips with her were always great, and I looked forward to my getaways. I was coming to find out more and more how much I loved having the space and opportunity to go away on my own, away from my family. It had nothing to do with them personally. It actually is just part of who I am—I am a solo explorer, who also enjoys venturing out with others as well. I just need to change up my co-explorers depending on the adventure. It's how I travel and experience life best.

Soon after, my girlfriend left the company, and the trips I went on were not as fun anymore, though I was still grateful for the breaks away. I went to Atlantic City again, but that ended up being a hot mess, as I went with a pregnant (and sick) co-worker and landed myself in a kinda shady emergency room for a tetanus shot after the metal booth cut my hand. Anyone who knows me and how squeamish I am can just imagine what I put my poor co-worker through as I was wimping out on a gurney getting a simple shot (good times). It is an experience we both look back on now and laugh at—but one that we would never want to relive again together.

Later on, I got to experience Disney with another co-worker at a marketing conference in Orlando. I remember how cool it was to experience dinner at Emerils and taste my way through the different countries in Epcot with someone who truly appreciated the different cultures and foods. I also went on other trips with my bosses: one on a road trip through a snowstorm in Pennsylvania, and one to Las Vegas. You can imagine which one was more enjoyable.

Ah, Las Vegas. What was funny about this particular trip was that I had given my husband an "ultimatum" of sorts: before I would have any children, I wanted 3 more adventures: to go to Hawaii, to go on a cruise and to go to Las Vegas. The little trickster, once he learned that I was headed to Vegas for work, he counted that as one down. I had to give it to him; I didn't say that I had to go with him, so I had to let it count. But I have to say, it is not the same kind of experience going with a boss than it would be going

> We always took our day work seriously-but when off the clock, that was our time to enjoy the trip as we liked.

with your husband. But not in the way you would think. I swear, we got into Las Vegas, and my boss' eyes lit up like a little kid's in a candy shop. I soon assumed the adult role, and kept reminding him that we were in Vegas to do a trade show, and network. And what did he want to do? He wanted to book a helicopter ride over the Grand Canyon instead. Goodness gracious, looking back, I should have just let him do whatever he wanted and have his way.

Who on Earth tells their boss no, we can't go on such an incredible, possibly once-in-a-lifetime experience, on business time and money, because we needed to go set up a stupid booth and I needed to dress up like a monkey to entertain passersby? (One of our mascots. My debut into acting, perhaps? I'm trying to spin this in any positive light right now.)

I still can't believe I had turned that down. He probably would have done it too, and I am sure we would have figured out how to get everything done in time for the show. Instead, we ended up prepping everything, and then walking the strip, checking out the different casinos and had a nice dinner. So it definitely was not bad at all, and I got to experience a little bit of what Vegas had to offer—checking location one of three off my "before I have kids" list.

That was to be my last major business trip for a very long time. As the years went on, and I began having children, my job changed and my ability to explore dwindled. On very rare occasions now do I get to travel for business, and I will admit it has been very hard on me. Having children, and then later on becoming a single mom, it was difficult for me to get coverage to be able to go on business trips, so those opportunities became less available to me. I don't regret having my children, not in the least bit; but when I made the decision to have them, I had no idea the impact it would have upon my freedom and level of responsibility, and I would need to adapt to a brand new form of adventure.

There would only be a few more trips left for me before embarking on a path of isolation; one that would leave me without adventure, and without a sense of self. One where I put everyone else first, and denied any part of my creative, adventurous, free-spirited soul.

18. Dad and Disney: Hide the Kona Coffee

It had been such a long, long time since my family went on an actual vacation together, so my husband and I talked them into going to Disney World with us. Since none of them had ever been there, we led the party planning, and wanted to show them all of the things we loved most about it. We decided to stay at the Polynesian again, so that they could experience Tonga Toast and a Hawaiian atmosphere. And then we coordinated going to the different parks and dinner experiences and shows and character breakfasts—the whole nine yards.

It was definitely a unique trip, to say the least. While we were floating on cloud nine back in our playland, the diversity of family personalities decided to shine through. First, there was my dad, who became absolutely obsessed with Kona coffee to the point where I think he literally visited every possible bathroom in the parks as a result. That started stressing us out, having to stop all the time—he was worse than a child. It didn't help my already strained relationship with him, though I was grateful he chose coffee over alcohol this time. My parents would be fighting constantly about his coffee obsession (nothing new, just a different topic). We finally banned him from drinking the coffee altogether and encouraged him instead to purchase some to bring home and enjoy it there. Well, at least he could be easily persuaded.

And then there were my sisters, who I guess were at that age where not many things were cool, least of all, Disney. Here we were, in this magical world with these exquisitely detailed rides, and all I could hear was my one sister complaining how there were no thrill rides. She had zero appreciation for anything around her. She didn't want to go on the simple rides, was bored with the shows and couldn't even find a character to pretend to like. My mom had to calm both of us down several times because we were going at it constantly, the biggest blowout being in Epcot. If "baby rides" weren't bad enough, the torment she clearly conveyed over walking around "stupid countries" prompted a loud argument right outside of the aquarium—a place I figured she would find some level of happiness at because she loved everything to do with animals—but she couldn't enjoy even that.

To this day, I remember my mother begging me to just let it go and not let it ruin my time there, or hers. With some pouting and a little reluctance on both of our parts, we finally decided to stop fighting, for her sake. You'd think we were 5-year-olds all over again the way we constantly bickered.

Bless my mother for being the peacekeeper during this trip. She isn't a big fan to begin with of walking through theme parks, and then on top of that, she had to deal with fighting daughters and a pain in the ass husband. But at least I was able to experience the joy of seeing her eyes light up with wonder at everything she was experiencing. Although my sisters weren't big fans, my mother absolutely loved walking around the little countries in Epcot. I knew secretly she was a traveler at heart, and she really enjoyed it there. She would stop and look around the little marketplaces and dance to the music. I think it was her favorite place out of all of the parks.

And even though she was such a joyful spirit as we went through all of these different places, she didn't love everything about the trip; we were little rascals to her at times (outside of the fighting).

> *Had any of us realized that this would be our last vacation ever together as a family...*

Knowing she wasn't a fan of scary rides, we tricked her into going on the Dinosaur ride, and to this day we still laugh over the picture we bought of her terrorized face as the dinosaurs jumped out at her. Best picture ever. Not the best way to treat your peacekeeper; but she had a really good sense of humor about it after the fact as she threatened our lives enough that we would never pull that kind of stunt on her again. Like ever.

And then there was my husband, bless him too, for finding ways to keep bringing me back to my joy there whenever something frustrated me. Ever my Peter Pan, he would whisk me away to something fun to take my mind off the stress...usually to my favorite tiki room or a show nearby. A vacation was not supposed to be stressful, and he was determined to make sure that we got to enjoy it. I mean, there were moments we really had a blast together as a family, but I never realized how challenging a vacation like this would be, with so many different personalities and preferences.

There was my dad who just couldn't stop drinking coffee and driving us all insane; my then-saint-of-a-husband co-peacemaking with my mom to break up family fights; my one sister who hated everything because all she wanted were thrill rides; my other sister who didn't complain as much but also wished there were more thrill rides (thank God for a day at Universal/Islands of Adventure to restore sanity); my mom who was truly trying to enjoy everything but hated thrill rides and animals; and then there was me, who just wanted everyone to love the place as much as I did. Ah, can't win them all.

Butterfly Travels

My mom, sisters and I have been back together there since, with my kids, and the dynamics were completely different, and we all had a blast. Age (and kids) can do that for you. But had any of us realized that this would be our last vacation together ever as a complete family, perhaps we would have not spent so much time arguing, being bossy, being ungrateful and being so intolerant of each other. We would have treasured what would be our last memory together before the family broke apart. Luckily, we have learned from that, and now spend our vacations together with appreciation, acceptance and extra planning to ensure that everyone gets to do something they love. In fact…we are ready for our next family Disney adventure as I write this!

19. Tracing My Irish Roots

I love all my adventures. But hands down, one of the best journeys ever of my entire life (to date) was my trip to Ireland with my sister. I could write about this trip for pages. Because it wasn't just any old trip; it was engrossed with deep meaning, connection and soul awakening.

The decision to go to Ireland was inspired by my sister and our desire to uncover a family mystery. Before our grandmother passed, she alluded to a deep, dark secret of hers, and we were led to believe the key to unraveling it was in a small church near the home where our great-grandmother, her mother, lived back in Ireland. We were completely fascinated by the idea of discovering family history there, so we set off on an adventure to explore our roots in County Mayo.

What really made Ireland special for us was that we still had family over there that we had never met. Our ancestors came from an extremely large family; some came to America, some stayed in Ireland; but most who were still alive stayed in touch. So we connected with our grandmother's cousin, who happened to be a nun. What a wonderful woman, opening up a room at the convent for us to stay (that is an interesting story in itself!), and taking time off to be our personal tour guide throughout what is still to me the most beautiful country there ever was. A country that I instantly felt a strong connection to; I had been there before, and there was no doubt the Irish/Celtic culture ran deep in my blood, and in my

> **The super-sleuths were on a mission!**

soul lines. I had expected this kind of connection when I had ventured to Germany years earlier; but I was not surprised that Ireland called to me so profoundly, and continues to call me back.

Our trip started out with meeting other wonderful members of our family, and "enjoying" a traditional Irish breakfast. (Note to us and others: pudding is NOT a yummy dessert there.) Her brother was a priest and head of his church, so we also visited with him and toured his church grounds, which were beautiful. The irony at this point was that both of us at this time had denounced our Catholic faith, and weren't very spiritual at all, my sister more so, so we relied upon our well-bred good manners to be courteous and feign interest in all of these religious tours. And the fact that either of us with our potty mouths and well, carefree lives shall we say, were staying in a convent, was something that our family and friends back home were definitely having a giggle about. But I will say, it really was a lovely place, and all of the nuns were kind and gracious. We honestly wouldn't get better service at any hotel in any part of the world.

After meeting up with family, our cousin then took us on a road trip all around the region. We visited the Cliffs of Moher, our Lady of Knock (yes, another church) and went into town to the sweetest little village of shops. She also took us on a tour of our ancestral graveyards, where she lovingly explained the history of all of our roots. It really amazed me at how connected our elders really are to their elders, and how much our generation has lost contact or even desire with that level of connection and wisdom. We also learned about our royal heritage (which, of course, somewhere down the line, someone in our family ancestry had pissed someone important off and had our particular line disowned).

We later were taken to our great-grandmother's childhood home, which our cousins still owned and maintained. We sat by the fireplace while she told us even more stories about our family, how she grew up, what she knew, the history of the house. My sister and I were completely mesmerized by this whole experience. Then we got to go to sleep in the rooms our great-grandmother and her siblings slept in, and it was really cool! But admittedly, also a bit scary, as both of us felt the presence of a few spirits here and there roaming about. No doubt they were past relatives checking in on us!

The next morning, we were given the chance to go off on our own to explore our ancestors' childhood town…and track down that church. The super-sleuths were on a mission! We found it, and it was the sweetest little church, with these beautiful glass-stained windows. Being that our grandmother was still very sick back home, we lit a candle and said a prayer, and then collected some holy water to bring home to her, hoping in some way it would heal her. We then put on our detective "hats" and went exploring around the church and the area to see if we could uncover some kind of mystery.

It led us to a barren creek, and what seemed to be a dead end. We had thought for sure we would find some kind of answers in the house, town or church that would reveal a big secret. It was a bit disappointing. But realizing that we were not going to find anything, we did the next best thing: we imagined what our great-grandmother did along the creek when she was little, and made up our own fun stories about what life was like back then. How they did the wash right here, how they skipped rocks over the rushing water, or took an afternoon swim. It was fun to imagine what the times were like back then.

After we enjoyed some more time at our family home, we went off on more explorations of Ireland. Our cousin joined us in a dinner celebration at the Bunratty Castle, where we were whisked back to ancient times with music, dancing, stories and miel—an extremely delicious beverage that even our cousin enjoyed. (We actually think she is the coolest nun to ever exist on this planet). She then sent us on a journey cross-country to Dublin, where her other sister and family lived. They also graciously welcomed us into their home, and there we got to visit authentic pubs, the Guinness Factory and other city sites. Our journey then came to an end as we traveled back west and got on the plane to head home.

The feelings my sister and I were left with were truly unexplainable. Yes, it was a trip full of cultural exploration, family connectedness and definitely relaxation and hospitality. But for us, it was so much more. It had changed us. It gave us a deeper understanding of our roots. We both felt the connection to our past, and took that home with us. It strengthened our own relationship, as we had both become adults, and finally took that time to really bond with each other. For me, it anchored part of my soul and activated something within my heart. A fire that needed to burn, but that was yet to be uncovered. I could feel it. I still feel it. One day I need to go back there. In fact, we want to buy our ancestors' childhood home so that the history lives on for future generations—something that not many people can say nowadays.

20. Who Moved My Chi Chi? A Hawaiian Getaway

My husband was a pretty clever individual. Remember that "ultimatum" that I needed to go to Vegas, Hawaii and on a cruise before starting a family? Well, Vegas was covered. So this little genius decided for Christmas to book me a Hawaiian cruise—two in one shot. He got me there—again! It was to be a week-long cruise around all of the Islands. It was so exciting to plan all the different excursions we would go on; it was such a dream come true.

But like with everything else in our lives during that time, it really was too good to be true. One week before we were to set sail, the cruise ship company went bankrupt. Even though we had purchased insurance, there were no refunds. Bankruptcy was not covered. The very last voyage was the one before ours; if only they had held out one more week! But they didn't. You can imagine my devastation and anger. We had invested a lot of money into this trip, and we were completely screwed. We still had our flights out there, but no cruise. A cruise that covered our overnight stays and our meals. And all we had left was a budget for excursions and souvenirs.

I frantically looked for cheap hotels in Waikiki where we could stay for the week. We were saddened, wondering what on earth we could actually do besides sit on the beach with such a low budget. I really didn't even want to go at this point, but we had already planned the first night in a nice hotel (before the cruise departed) and a stopover in Disneyland in California on the way back, so we decided that we could just figure out the in between and make the best of it.

What appeared to be a "tragedy vacation" actually turned out to be a blessing in disguise. The hotel we stayed at was not the best, but it was clean, friendly and quiet. As we explored our area, we came across this little outside grill, where we were introduced to chi chis (pina coladas with vodka instead of rum), teriyaki chicken and a wonderful artist who sang and played his guitar acoustically, who we really enjoyed. It actually became our night spot for most of the week, as we completely fell in love with "our place." The rest of the week, we had managed to save up enough money to do some exploration of the island. We went on a cultural bus tour to see some interesting sites, such as the Dole plantation, learned about the history of the volcanoes and people, and each received our own cocoai beaded necklaces.

We also enjoyed an authentic luau. It was definitely not the experience I expected it to be. We thought we would love the food, but seeing and then eating the smoked piggy and tasting the acclaimed purple poi didn't really live up to our culinary expectations. But at least the chi chis were flowing! We did get to see some traditional hula dancing and get a lesson in it, which was pretty cool. But mostly, it was just about being together, the rest of the world and worries away from us, and enjoying the beautiful, calm surroundings. You can't be in Hawaii and not feel blissful; even when your whole vacation world was turned upside down.

We had both agreed that had we actually went on the cruise, we would have been exhausted and not really enjoyed what the big island—or any of the islands—had to offer. We'd have a booked up itinerary of seeing this and that, and honestly, the trip we ended up having was so much more connecting by being forced to enjoy the simpler places and activities—and each other. It was the honeymoon we never had, and we were closer than ever after that trip. This was the trip that taught me that planning is not everything; and that in every disaster, there is a blessing and a lesson. It was probably the universe's first profound teaching of surrender for me, since I was fighting it so hard with anger. But once I just allowed this experience in, it ended up being an extremely memorable and special time.

Of course, on the way back, we did our stopover for two days in LA for some Disneyland and California Adventure action. It was such a different vibe than in Florida, and we both really enjoyed it so much more. Relaxed and happy, we navigated through both parks at a slower pace, taking it all in instead of the usual rush to see everything. There was just something about that place that made me smile—and it was more than it being Disney-related. I had no idea then that my first taste, and love, of California would soon completely capture my heart, soul and attention a few years down the road.

21. A Dry Spell and a Dry Heart

After Hawaii, we went to a few more places, nothing too exciting or memorable, with the exception of the Disney Cruise out of Florida. (I got my separate cruise still!) We really enjoyed that trip—and the repeat cruise trip a year later with his parents when I was pregnant with our first child. We had booked that trip as an anniversary present to his parents, long before I ended up pregnant. That was to be the last trip we (I) would take for a very, very long time.

Talking about this time in my life is quite painful. Within a few years' time, I experienced a tremendous amount of loss that catapulted me into my darkest hours. It began when my parents had decided to finally split up. My mother approached me about buying the family home, half in an effort to help us financially, and half in an effort to help her and my sisters stay in the house. My husband and I had felt the pressure of needing to save the house, and my family, from this marital fallout. It was all anyone had left of our memories and childhood, and none of us were ready to let it all go. So, reluctantly we agreed, and that's when the family disintegration began.

As my dad was getting ready to leave the house for the last time, after signing the deed over to me, I had given him a little present to help him in his new home. It was intended to be a loving gesture on my part to show my support, but it wasn't exactly received that way, and his reaction was one of hurt. Words were exchanged, and

> *This was a major turning point in my life. I was at an all-time low.*

that moment became the ultimate end for me. I had already suffered enough throughout childhood with the ramifications of his drinking and emotional abandonment. Putting that aside, I was trying to reach out to him during this difficult time, to only be shut down. That was my final breaking point—and I let him know as much. When he left that house, he never came back. He was only supposed to be leaving my mother, not all of us. My sisters tried keeping a relationship with him, but I was completely turned off by then by his lack of interest in me, and I chose to disown him. He no longer existed in my eyes, and my heart turned cold.

A lifetime of anger and resentment bubbled up and began taking over my life, my emotions and my entire soul. And one by one, more walls came crashing down. I thought we would be financially secure, but a bomb was dropped on us and we were never able to recover. My beloved Nanny passed, and the grief of already losing her to Alzheimer's only deepened as I realized I lost the one person in this entire world who ever truly understood me. It was completely unbearable, and the darkness just kept enveloping me—to the point where I could not even embrace the blessing of the greatest joy in my life: motherhood.

Although there was genuine, exquisite awe in welcoming my daughter into the world, and it was a new type of blessing and adventure itself, being confined to my home while my husband still traveled for work ate away at me little by little. I had built up an enormous resentment over me having to live in that house and take on the additional responsibility while he still had his freedom to get away on his weekly wrestling gigs. Even though it was his living, it still bothered me that he had that flexibility and I didn't.

Jennifer Watson

I was never one to be a homebody, but that is what I had become. I took my daughter on little outings, but my overprotective nature and paranoia kept me from venturing out too often. I became a recluse, declining social invitations, unable to attend work functions requiring travel, and we were too broke to go on any type of vacation. Life was definitely headed in a downward spiral. Soon after, my Poppy joined Nanny in Heaven, and all of this grief became overwhelming.

I tried to pep life up a bit with a few trips here and there, but nothing really sparked my love of adventure anymore. Not even a trip to Las Vegas with my mom. Although it was nice to spend some bonding time with her, the whole time I was worried about my daughter because she was so young and missed me, and my husband didn't have too much of a clue about how to handle a baby. (He admittedly is more comfortable relating to and caring for older children who are less dependent.) So I couldn't let go and just have a fun time, as much as my mom tried to comfort me. And that was it for me. I decided I couldn't ever leave my child like that again.

Instead, I left my entire extended family and moved to Pennsylvania. We just could no longer afford to live in New York anymore. And that seemed to be the perfect place, since I was still able to work from home there and partially commute with my job, and it wasn't too far away from my family that I couldn't see them as often as I wanted to. His parents had moved up with us, so I had that extra support with my daughter in case I needed to go to Long Island for work and didn't want to bring her, or had errands to run, or just needed a little break. I had hoped that life could perhaps turn back around for us, and that the nagging feeling in my stomach about our own failing marriage would subside without all of this added stress. It was actually the ideal situation—on paper.

But Pennsylvania turned out to be the worst adventure of my life. I truly became a bonafide hermit, and only went out to Walmart on the weekends. That was my big excitement in life. As soon as we moved there, my husband was offered what supposedly was a training opportunity in Texas, leaving me and my daughter alone for three months. With only a few days notice, my little girl and I ended up secluded in this new state and barren home with no friends and only his parents to talk to. The depression and reclusion only worsened, and I no longer recognized the lifeless woman looking back at me in the mirror. The worst part was I just didn't care.

As the financial stress grew stronger, and the fights got tougher, I couldn't take society in general anymore and I pulled away from my family and friends completely. I could not care less about how sloppily I dressed, my growing weight, if I wore makeup or who saw me like that in public. I had no pride in my appearance, my attitude—in anything—except having a spotless house. Our relationship was rapidly falling apart; he would leave to go to side work and I would be stuck at home constantly. We never had any money to do anything, not even to go to a local concert or out to a decent dinner. There were no more dates. No more trips, outside of the long drive back and forth to work every other week. There was nothing. Nothing but this huge isolated house among snowy mountains and never-ending woods that I had grown to hate.

We did attempt a trip after his Texas jaunt to DisneyWorld to fulfill our dream of taking our daughter there. And although nothing could take away the joy of seeing how precious she was in this land of magic, it felt like it was still just the two of us, with some man who had become a detached outsider. I choose not to get into the deeper details of this depressive time in my life, but needless to say, this was a major turning point for me. I was at an all-time low. No self-worth; no family and friend connections;

no marital connections. Having my son during this time was the biggest miracle of my life. I still thank God to this day for granting my wish, and for being so merciful about it.

By the time he was born, rock bottom had arrived. Looking back now, I recognize that on top of everything, I was suffering from postpartum depression. But my time in isolation was about to come to an end. Everything exploded into a divorce, and I just didn't know if I could take anymore heartache. I had no idea how the hell I was going to pull off being alone, raising two kids pretty much on my own, with little physical support and under dire financial circumstances. I just knew I had to do it—if not for my sake, then for the sake of those two precious babies.

I can still to this day remember that instance I came up for air and took control back of my own life. I looked in the mirror at the tear-stained, bloated, soul-less eyed face and said to myself, Enough. I decided then and there that I was headed back to New York, to my home, to my family and friends (whoever would accept me back), and that this was not the end of my life. This was just the beginning, and dammit, I was no longer a victim. I never was; I simply was just a drama queen playing a role for the sympathy and attention. "Look at what he did to me" solicited much more support than "Look at what I've done to myself." That was all about to change, and with that declaration, a new Jennifer was born.

After a rather civil divorce agreement and proceeding, I left Pennsylvania behind, foreclosing on the house and never looking back. It took some time, and a lot of healing, patience and compassion, but I had to put all of my pain aside for my children and make their physical, emotional and psychological needs my priority. I would not have them affected by the decisions of their parents, nor would depression reign supreme over their (our) lives. My dry spell was finally over, and life was about to renew itself.

22. To Saturn and Back: An Energetic Journey

After moving back, there was a huge healing process that I was about to begin. I hadn't recognized at the time that part of my self-destruction and depression was due to ignoring my innate sense of adventure. I had always thirsted for knowledge in the form of school, travel and reading: all of which had been denied during the last few years. But I had not uncovered that—yet.

What I did uncover was the resurgence of a curiosity I had always had: astrology. I was connected to a website through an old high school friend of mine, and immediately was hooked on learning everything I could about what astrology was really all about. Then I had my first chart reading, which completely blew me away. This man had described me to a tee, and then revealed things about me that I at first rejected as nonsense, yet heard my soul cry out, yes! Yes, finally, you recognize that I am a part of you!

It just so happened that I was going through what is termed a Saturn return, followed by Saturn in my sun. For those who do not know astrology, it is a point in time where the energies of the planets basically go into your life and force you to evaluate what works and what doesn't, and if it doesn't and you ignore it, the universe will remove it anyway—sometimes without mercy. And that is exactly what had happened to me. What I had closed my eyes to and ignored was blatantly thrown right into my face so that I could no longer live in denial. And beginning to understand that, and learning the true meaning of gratitude, lessons and faith,

I began to come out of my isolated coma and back into the world. My healing had begun, and I took it on with full force. I tried to read every book I could on astrology so that I could understand my chart—and myself—better. I met so many wonderful people online, and their wisdom, love and support shifted my whole perspective on life. I was able to reconnect with old friends who surprisingly stood by my side, forgiving me for my withdrawal, and my family embraced me back with excitement that I had returned.

Life was still a struggle; getting a divorce, figuring out child support, letting go of the impact a foreclosure has on your perfect credit score, and trying to figure out how to raise two children completely on your own was no easy task. But somehow, with all of this positive energy and healing tools behind me, I was beginning to let go of all of the blame I put on others and accept responsibility for my own feelings, actions and expectations. I was introduced to the concept of "forgiveness"—and that changed everything for me.

Having this new source of inspiration and wisdom created a spark that had long been doused in me. I wanted to know more about the planets, and all of these different concepts of spirituality that I heard about. I felt like I was really stepping into my power. The wisdom from my reading, and my new mentor, helped me to see that my life was a big adventure. That all those feelings I had when I was in a spotlight as a wrestler's girlfriend, and that my desire to help others was more than just a dream, but a purpose; that loving my self was the most profound thing that I could do for me and my children, as this was all part of who I was, and who I needed to be.

Navigating these new self-empowerment waters was tricky. Relationships were put to the test. I pushed boundaries—my own, and others'. I think it is natural after any extreme life transition that imbalance and rebellion occurs, and that's what I was experiencing. After being a hermit for so long, my social life became a huge priority for me—as did men. In my quest for self-worth, I sought validation in the wrong places. I was struggling with the morals and values I was brought up with, and the new, independent beliefs that were developing within me. I cared a lot about my appearance, experimenting with darker hair and sexier clothing, now that the stress of a divorce and move somehow triggered a weight loss of over 70 pounds. I felt beautiful again, something I had not felt in a very, very long time.

I was a walking dichotomy as I went through this energetic adventure. I would be peaceful (for the most part) with my ex, because I was committed to not being vengeful in any way; I refused to have my children grow up in a broken home where the parents were always at odds with each other, or badmouthing each other. I made sure both of them were in therapy to get the professional help that I could not provide so that they adapted to this new life in an emotionally stable way. Every action I took where they were concerned was to ensure they never felt unloved, blamed, unsupported or unstable; and so far, it's worked.

But on the flip side, when it came to me, the healing rollercoaster unraveled behavioral traits that weren't necessarily accepted, but critical to my self-discovery. Sometimes a walk on the dark side is exactly what we need to see—and embrace—our true light. I am extremely grateful for every single lesson my Saturn transits taught me, even the most difficult of ones. I am glad to have gone through everything that I had went through. I regret nothing. This energetic (and spiritual) journey awakened me to the source of who I was; the source of my pains and my patterns; the doors to my passions and my purposes; the depth of my ability to forgive and to love, despite character flaws; the unlimited amount of my own strength, courage and resilience; to the acceptance of the light and the dark within me, and to the realization that I was a powerful being. A being whose destiny is love, adventure and inspiration; a destiny that would never be denied again.

Saturn Rain

It's been raining for what seems like years

The rain can be dark and cold, it can bring gloom and great sadness, yearning for the sun to shine again

But do not look upon rain as this cloud of negativity or despair, and see it for what it truly is

Without rain, we would not learn how to appreciate the sun and all its glory

Without the clouds, there would be no clearing after the storm

Without the thunder, we would not awake to see the lightening strike a new beginning

Rain is growth, for you need both water and sunlight to survive

It washes away the past and cleanses the present to make way for the future

It only washes away the debris; never a strong foundation from which to rebuild upon

It can rain for days on end, forcing us to go inside, to face the debris of our lives and let it go

It is then we can walk freely outside, and turn our face up to the drizzling sky with courage

Letting the rain pour down on us, feeling the freedom of each drop as we release our fears

*And only after accepting the beauty of rain
and remembering the sun will come out again*

*We are graced with the beauty of the rainbow,
its miracle of colors and grandeur*

*A lesson has been learned, with the promise
of a new day, a new life and a new hope*

*I say let it rain, and rain hard, so that I can bask in the sunlight
of my tomorrow, which shall become my today*

23. Sisterly Bonds at the Jersey Shore

My very first adventure as a single woman was a trip I took with my sisters down to the Jersey Shore. It had been years since we truly did anything as sisters, so when my ex happened to have the kids for an extended weekend, we planned a weekend getaway for some days in the sun, and some nights in the clubs. To be honest, I swear I was younger than them at the time with the way I was acting. Since I was such a golden girl who followed the rules all my life, I missed out on a bit of the growing up debauchery and rebellion, and decided to make up for lost times. I was smart enough to be an adult during the day, taking my job and motherhood responsibilities seriously, but once the sun went down and the kids were soundly tucked away in bed, out came my alter ego and the partying began.

In fact, we were leaving very early in the morning, but that still didn't keep me from going out the night before and not returning until a few hours before departure. I had complete freedom from any responsibility, and I intended to let loose and have a good time. A few drinks, some dancing, some flirting—all pretty harmless, but to some, I might have been a little too "old" for it—or worse: a mother should not do such things (as if becoming a mother meant I stopped being a full-blooded woman). Ah, whatever, we all have those periods in our life where we have lost our way on purpose. For me, it happened to be in my thirties instead of my teens or twenties.

Whatever my nightly adventure, I was still ready to go for a weekend of sisterly love by the time the car pulled up to my front door. The car ride was so fun, listening to music, singing and laughing with each other. We were so excited for some time away from every day life, because their lives were no bowl of cherries at that point either. What was really nice was that we were able to get into deep conversations like we never had before. There is a pretty large age gap between me and them, with them being closer in age, so I always felt a little outside of that bond. But we all connected as adults now, talking freely about life, boys, sex and all kinds of "taboo" topics that were finally safe for me to talk about.

Along with learning about forgiveness and self-awareness, I was learning how to let go of judgments and be more open-minded to the world around me. For so long, I had been stuck on old fashioned thinking, with very little knowledge of life in general, and my hermit years sure didn't help that. But boy, was my first year of divorce a huge eye opener to what the world was like, good and bad, and all of the possibilities that were out there.

We had a blast laying on the beach, having some drinks while catching the rays and chatting some more. We went shopping on the boardwalk and all decided that we deserved some cute new outfits, so we each bought either a shirt or dress to wear out that night. We got dolled up and headed out for a night of dancing. Now with three rather adorable blonde sisters, a few drinks and booties that don't stop, we were in for a great night of drama. Much laughter, some tears, some hookups, some falling down on the beer-drenched floors, some stalker avoiding—all making for a memorable night out that yes, we did all in fact, remember.

The next day, I was in bit of a "rebellious" mood, at least what to me, was rebellious for my personality. I am not much into

> *It's hard to look at these things within yourself, but I'd much rather recognize it and shift it than allow it to lay dormant.*

piercings and tattoos, and in the past had been a bit of a snob with the eye-rolls whenever my sisters, ex-husband or anyone else talked about permanently altering their bodies. As part of my deciding to give up the homeless old woman look and actually take pride in myself, I thought now was the time to start wearing jewelry again—and that included earrings.

I forgot how much fun earrings and other accessories were! So on the Boardwalk, I went and got my ears re-pierced since my first holes had closed up over the years from neglect. The prospect of getting to buy, coordinate and wear earrings was really exciting—it's the simple things, folks! And then as we continued to walk along the boardwalk, I decided to get—GASP—a temporary tattoo. (Told you I was a rebel.) Something I thought I would never, ever do permanently. So I had them design hearts with my kids' initials in them for my back left shoulder, and even though it wasn't very creative on the spot, it did leave me feeling a bit sexy, and understanding why people chose to get tattoos.

I get that sometimes there is deep meaning, and other times it is just whimsical. And by getting a temporary one myself, I was able to shift my perspective to be more open-minded and less critical of others. Not that I maliciously intended to look down on anyone for any reason, but at times in my life, I really did scowl at things that I would not approve of for myself. That was definitely an important awareness and breakthrough I encountered often after my divorce. It's hard to look at these things within yourself, but I'd much rather recognize it and shift it than allow it to lay dormant.

So now, I have a great appreciation for body artwork, and honor the individuality that it represents. I may never choose to get a tattoo, or get another ear piercing, but I certainly no longer judge others for their right to freedom of self-expression. And in the process of learning this, I got to sport a cool image on my shoulder for a little bit as I stepped outside of my comfort zone.

That seemed to be the norm for this trip, as I learned so much, and from my little sisters, no less. Clearly, age does not indicate wisdom and knowledge, and I appreciated everything my sisters had to share with me and teach me. It was nice to get away from the pain for a while, and to do it safely with two women I love most in this world. Two women who had my back, as I had theirs. Who didn't judge me, and who I finally did not judge back. I had been so tough on them as the incessant goody-goody, and this was my chance to just be me, and let them be them, and acceptance and love was pretty much the theme of the weekend.

You know the saying that chance made us sisters, hearts made us friends? Well, I was damn lucky to not have been blessed with just one sister, but two. And the true potential of that gift was really revealed to me that weekend, and the words my mother had always said to us finally made sense: "One day, you will all be grateful to have each other as sisters. You may fight and bicker and disagree now, and even hate each other as you grow up. But one day you will realize what a blessing it is to have sisters by your side."

And for the three of us, that day had come. We might have been hot messes as we tore up the Jersey Shore, but we did it together, and it had bonded us for life. And years later, as we have outgrown the party lifestyle and stepped into the truth of our selves and our lives, our bond has only become stronger. That weekend cemented our sisterhood, and I will never forget feeling like I finally belonged as one of them.

24. What Happens in AC, Doesn't Always Stay There (Part 1)

Well, once I got a taste of the girls weekend out type of adventure with my sisters, I didn't hesitate to join in the fun on an invitation to a Bachelorette overnight party in Atlantic City. I mean, who can resist an all-night adventure with some of your best girlfriends in a place like that?

It started out with an interesting car ride of stops and starts and traffic and anxiousness to just get there. We were ready to check-in, get something to eat and get our party on. We quickly freshened up and then met up with our darling bachelorette and crew in a kickass suite where we began the pictures, laughs and drinks. We then headed down to one bar that had amazing martini concoctions, and a dance floor that called our name. Of course, that led to some bar hopping and other dancing, and some chance encounters.

I'll never forget this one guy we met down there, "MJ." Well, even if I wanted to forget, my girlfriends still to this day love to remind me about him. Being new to the dating and social scene again, I liked the attention of being the only blonde in the entire group, and used that to my advantage. Now somewhere throughout the course of the evening, I had this notion that it would be a good idea to hook-up with this guy in the hallway near our rooms. My one girlfriend—sober, clever and up $1200 from a slot machine encounter—went to bed and threatened my life (in a sense) if I even thought about bringing him back up to our shared room.

Well, even with a few drinks in me, I knew enough to respect my friend, and second guess what I was doing. Luckily, I didn't have the opportunity to show poor judgment, because this guy's group of friends were about to leave on a bus, and although torn between me and a bus ride home, he opted to not be stranded.

Of course, that didn't set too well with me, and I felt rejected. Oh alcohol, you vicious self-esteem killer. So there I was, in a hotel not knowing honestly where the hell I was—and worse—where the hell any of my friends were. Tears streaming down my face, I thought it might be a good idea to try to find them. Down I went to the main scene, determined to find someone—anyone—that I knew. That's when I pulled out my phone—at 1am—and pressed the name to call the friend I wanted to find, only to have one of my bosses pick up the phone and ask "Who the hell is this?"

Yeah, that happened. My finger slipped, and her name was right next to my friend's name. So I quickly hung up, went into a bit of domino-like hysterics over calling my boss and thinking I was going to be fired, being "rejected" by MJ, and not knowing where my friends were. Thankfully, I found one and she happily guided me to the others, as she humored my drunk ass and got me to finally stop crying. Whew! (Oh and by the way, I did confess to my boss that Monday that it was me who had accidentally called her, and she ended up laughing hysterically about it.)

When I caught up with my friends, they were hanging out with a co-worker who just happened to be down there at the same time with his friends, and they were gambling for a little bit. We stayed there for a while, but then we had the urge to do some more dancing, and wound up at this really fun Cuban club, where we closed out the bar, and the night, in the wee hours of the morning before we hit the sheets.

Now, why in the world is she revealing all of this to us, you might think. Well, my friends, it's not a story that was kept private, so why not share? I'm certainly not allowed to forget it! I mean, I guess it didn't pan out with that guy because I wasn't actually on the bus, otherwise, given my transportation history, the story might have turned out much differently. But I have to say that even with the messed up hookup, some additional drama and fighting amongst this diverse group of girls (I plead guilty to cattiness) and getting a wee bit lost while calling my boss after-hours, it was a really great night of girl bonding.

We laughed, we danced and really connected. It was the first time in a really long time, aside from the weekend with my sisters, where I truly felt the spirit of friendship. After cooping myself up for so long, going into depression, and pulling away from these very same girls I was celebrating with, I realized the power of friendship. No matter what happens in your life, you can always go back home, where the people who truly love you for who you are, are willing to wait for you to find yourself, and welcome you back with open arms—and with photos of you hugging a man you thought was an "8" who was anything but.

25. Owning my Loneliness: Bahama Seclusion

The trip with my sisters and friends shortly after returning home to a newly divorced life in New York opened up a Pandora's box for me. The travel bug was back, and it bit me hard. It was a struggle adjusting to being a single mom, especially when their dad lived in another state and I had hardly any physical support from him. I was pretty much on my own to hold down a full-time job, raise them, take them to school/daycare and navigate through the most painful time of my life without letting it affect them. The pressure was mounting, and I was feeling a bit claustrophobic. I always had the need in me for "alone time"; it was why I was so flexible about my husband traveling for work, because it both gave us space. Ideally, it should have been a perfect set-up.

But now in this role, with very little time for myself and sitter costs eating up my bank account for work and happy hour excursions, I needed a real kind of break. Not one to just party the night away for a few hours. I needed time away to think, heal and just be by myself for a while. Luckily, my mom had offered to watch the kids so I could go away for a few days by myself to the Bahamas, and peacefully, knowing they were safe and in good hands. She knew I needed this time away to re-evaluate my life, and find some clarity about how to live it.

When I would tell people I was going away by myself, I got the weirdest looks. Why wasn't anyone going with you, at least a friend? I would get asked. Not many could understand my need

> *This cycle had to stop. I was not going to let depression take over my life again.*

for solitude after everything I was working through, but I knew in my heart it was something I had to do for myself.

So I booked one of those all-inclusives during a spring break (and you can imagine what happened when I realized that I didn't have the foresight to plan outside of college spring break). But I was only going for a couple of days, and I needed some beach time and a relaxed nightlife. When I got there, everything was perfect. The weather was gorgeous, the service was friendly, the room was amazing and it was really nice to just spend some quiet time to myself. I thought, wow, this is exactly what I needed. This was going to be the perfect trip.

But then night time came. And the nights there were no different than the nights at home—except, it was more obvious how alone I was in this world while I was there. At least at home, I had a reason to be alone, as my children were tucked snug in their beds and I couldn't go anywhere. But here, there was nightlife; people to meet; fun to be had. I couldn't bear to deal with any of it. I tried to sit out in the main lounge where others were, but quickly I ended up in my room, crying my eyes out. I called my mother, completely bawling. I was utterly depressed. There—I finally realized it and admitted it out loud. All of my acting out was a result of my postpartum depression turned full-on depression, and my inability to cope with the pain of the divorce, the pangs of loneliness and the devastation of multiple rejections. I was in paradise, and I could not find an ounce of happiness.

Thank goodness for my mother during this time. I knew her heart was breaking—and had been breaking—for me throughout this whole transition. She had some very motherly things to say, and then some more uplifting ones. Words that gave me the courage to sleep it off that night, and wake up anew tomorrow and enjoy the opportunity in front of me. And that was all I needed to hear. I just needed to acknowledge my emotional demons, and then confront them. I was not a victim, remember? This cycle had to stop. I was not going to let depression take over my life ever again. I was not going to let my wounds stop me from fulfilling some bucket-list opportunities.

I had already booked an off-site adventure before I arrived, filled with activities I have never done before. I went all out, and I was not about to let my fears and anxieties stop me from what I intended to accomplish. I had a deep-seated fear of the water. I always worried about drowning, so I had denounced any form of swimming or water enjoyment outside of safely contained bubble baths. But this trip was about breaking through those fears. And once I woke up in the morning, I took my mother's advice and decided to face them head on with all the courage I had within me.

First up was snorkeling. I know, way to break into things gently, right? Well when I decide to do something, I don't do it half-ass, or wade in the water. Literally. I get in a life jacket and jump overboard. (Okay, I actually walked slowly and hesitantly down the boat ladder, but that didn't sound as dramatic.) I almost didn't make it. I literally was petrified. I swam out a few feet and tried to look into the water. I had this snorkel mask on my face, and the fears bubbled up so violently inside of me that I began to hyperventilate. Literally, I could not breathe and had to pull the snorkel mask off. Immediately, I headed back and up into the boat. That was it. I tried it. I was done. No more.

But then as I stood there, watching others enjoy it and talk about the beautiful creatures they had seen, I felt the nagging in my stomach that I couldn't give up now. I don't know where I found the strength, but I did and I went back in. And this time, I allowed myself to breathe into a state of calmness, and then went under. I wasn't down for long, but I was down long enough to see what I was missing. The colors and the vibrance of sea life took my breath away—this time, in a good way. This feeling of pride swelled up inside of me in ways I can't even explain. I faced one of my deepest fears—the water—and not only did I survive, but I loved every minute of it.

So when it came time to move on to my next adventure of jet skiing—something I had actually done once before and liked—I was pretty fearless. Before, I had my husband and his family right next to me guiding me through the waters, since I was terrified. Not this time. This time, I hopped on that ski and rode out like the badass I was!

Then I headed straight out to try something else new: parasailing. That also frightened me a bit, but not because of the height. Being high in the air never bothered me. It was the potential landing into the water (and of course, drowning, because that happens on a guided tour with a lifejacket on, right?) that had my nerves shot. But I had just been snorkeling and jet skiing. So this was something I was ready to take on. And it was another amazing experience, being up in the sky, just gliding along and seeing how beautiful the earth was below. I felt such a sense of peace up there. I had conquered extreme fear. I had battled my previous night's depression. I had come so far from being that woman who held herself hostage in her own home for years. I was *free*.

After my excursions were over, it was time to head back to the resort—and time to face another night alone. I could feel the anxiety starting to bubble up as I faced eating dinner alone again and going back to my room alone again. I got my food and was about to actually disappear to my room, when I saw two women, gratefully closer in age to me than all of the college kids running around, walking down the stairs in front of me. I have no idea where I found the courage, but I called out to them and asked if they would mind if I joined them for dinner since I was there on my own.

That decision changed everything for me. They graciously accepted, and I had a wonderful dinner getting to know two incredible women who happened to also live in New York! What a great feeling of reaching out to strangers and finding a connection. We ended up going for a walk to the casinos that night together, then back to the hotel lounge. One girl wanted to go to bed, but the other one was willing to stay up with me for a little while longer. We really connected—and in fact, have stayed in touch and met up on other adventures since. We hung out again during the next day, as I prepared to leave later that evening, and it was nice not to feel so alone on my solo adventure.

It really is amazing how transformational one experience—three days—can be in your life. What started out as a very lonely, fearful, depressed journey ended up freeing me of so much emotional baggage I had. I overcame serious blocks and challenges—physically, mentally and socially. I opened the doors to meeting beautiful people, and seeing more of the world than if I had crawled back into my shell and back into my room. That trip changed my perspective, and opened up my heart a bit more. I wasn't so afraid to go it alone and take chances. It was brave enough of me to even consider going all the way to the Bahamas on my own; but to actually have significant life breakthroughs as part of that solo journey, was something I would take with me in how I sought adventure and opportunity for the rest of my life.

26. A Summit of Soulmates: A Californian Beginning

Never in a million years would I imagine the intensity of transformation I would undergo after my divorce, nor the paths it would lead me to, the doors that would open or the exploration of worlds unknown that I would encounter. You know that feeling when you just KNOW something is meant to be, or KNOW that you are meant to be connected to a certain person, and you just can't explain it? That was the feeling I got when I was introduced to the astrological website I mentioned earlier. One glance and the familiarity of it all was like a magnet, drawing me in to a destiny I was finally ready to uncover.

A whole new world was discovered. Wisdom. Healing. Mind expansion. International connections. Loving friendships. Technological advances. Inner discovery. I owe most of my enlightenment, awareness and healing to this community I became an integral part of. What was really cool about it was that it opened me up to the possibilities of unlimited adventure—and that's when I really started getting back into my love of traveling.

It all started out with an overseas friend making a journey out to California; the hub of where our loving community lay. I decided then and there that I, too, was going to make that journey, and together we began rallying for a summer summit: a meeting of all of these amazing people who worked alongside each other daily, but only knew each other electronically. I was able to not only manifest a cheap ticket out to Los Angeles thanks to an old friend of mine who worked for the airline, but I scored one as well for another girl who lived in Pennsylvania nearby state so that she could come out with me. She stayed at my house before we left, and we became instant friends. We felt like we had known each other forever, and were soon to find out that it would be the same feeling with just about everyone else we were about to meet on the West Coast.

I remember the moment we landed and I got into that rental car—I knew exactly where I was. I had been here before. Technically, yes, I was, on my way back from my Hawaii trip, but it wasn't that kind of familiarity. It was much, much deeper. I drove on the roads like I had driven them before. I knew where I was going, and if I got lost, I had an internal GPS that guided me right back to where I needed to be. There was a freedom in the air. An intense freedom that I could not even explain, but just felt to my core. There is this energy about California that to this day beckons to my soul; a deep calling that I am meant to be there.

I was only there for a three-day weekend, but it was among the most powerful weekends of my life. I met people from all over the world who I had email and/or phone conversations with, so when I saw them in person, it was just as if we were just finally catching up after not seeing each other for a while. It was mind-boggling how we all felt the same way. And everyone was every bit as kind, loving and genuine as they seemed to be. I was in complete awe of this collection of "lightworkers," and honored to be standing among them as a newbie.

But being a newbie, I felt the intensity of the energy, and began breaking down. Every insecurity, past and present, started to surface. In the beginning of the evening, it was only a few of us together for dinner, and it was so comfortable and natural. I felt loved and like I belonged, and it was just the perfect size for me to really feel safe. And then we moved onto the party, where more

> *There is an energy about California that to this day beckons to my soul; a deep calling that I am meant to be there.*

and more people began to join, and the once confident Jenny was starting to shrivel up into her shy Virgo in the corner defense mode. What made matters worse was as others kept drinking, I was getting more sober. And uncomfortable. Not because anyone made me feel that way, but because I started feeling once again, my old pattern, as if I did not belong there. I wasn't good enough. I was no longer shining with personalized attention, but just another person in the room. At one point, I had broken down crying, and a few people were kind enough to talk me through it until I felt a little better. And then since I was pegged trustworthy, and sober, I became the designated caretaker for a select few who were a little on the inebriated side.

The next morning, while everyone in my room was sleeping, I snuck outside to the balcony where the beautiful morning weather welcomed me with loving winds, and a shoulder to cry on. I don't know exactly what I was crying about, but I began bawling my eyes out. It felt like every ounce of pain within me wanted to be released, and as much as I wanted to control it so that no one in the room would wake up and see me, my emotions betrayed me and there was no stopping it. My one roomie found me and she brought me inside after she told our other roomie that I was crying. I was so angry because I didn't want him to know, or anyone to know, how weak I was being, or think I was always this emotional. But he insisted I come in and talk with him, as my new girlfriend stepped out for a bit.

That was a very difficult—but extremely healing—morning in my life. It had been a long time since I had been held in a man's arms, even platonically, and yet he lovingly held me as I cried, talked and shared my heart's pain with him. I covered everything from my childhood anger about my dad, to the dissolution of my marriage. And he just let me get it all out, allowing me to finally express my deepest vulnerabilities to someone, and not feel ashamed of it. Even though I was in therapy at the time, there was something much different about opening the deepest parts of your heart to someone outside of a professional setting.

He was so very kind and gentle about my feelings, helping me to see that holding on to all of this pain was hurting me more than if I would just let it all go. I had no idea that someone could be so loving and supportive, and that you could be so genuinely close with someone without any ulterior motives. Time had made me bitter against all men; my dad, my ex-husband, the few men who were more than willing to soothe me temporarily with casual, non-committal encounters.

But here, with this particular man, I felt safe. I felt unjudged, and truly cared about. He helped me see certain things about myself, and how I needed to release so many of these wounds and start loving myself. He helped me to realize that what I craved from men was not attention, but affection—and that this is what I deserved. It shifted my whole perspective and made me realize what I was blocking out of my life out of fear; fear of rejection and abandonment. From that moment on, a bond was formed and an awareness created, and I will forever be grateful for that heartfelt moment.

The rest of the weekend was filled with similar breakdowns and breakthroughs. I felt like it was a never-ending therapy session in a sense, as this intense healing went on. And not just with support from him, but also from a few of the other wonderful friends I had the opportunity to bond with over those next few days. I had forged strong friendships with these people I had just met overnight, yet somehow I knew our souls have known each other for many lifetimes, and were just waiting for the right time to meet up in this one. We enjoyed days at the beach, fun dinners, movie nights in, swims in the pool and deep conversations in the hot tub. Not only did I shed a lot of emotional baggage, but I allowed myself to let my guard down with these strangers and step outside of my comfort zone, letting the true me out without fear that what they saw would not be good enough; because with them, I was. And, without them, I came to realize, I also was.

There was such a sense of freedom and relief being there in California, in that environment of love, that I did not even want to go home. In fact, I had emailed one of my best friends at home to tell her just that. I just couldn't bear to tear myself away. I went for a walk one morning on my own, and asked for a sign. I felt in my gut that I wasn't ready to leave. I came across a little European café that reminded me of Spain, and I ordered what I had gotten oh so many times in my favorite one in Barcelona, and sat outside praying for guidance. I kept feeling my Nanny's presence, and was reminded of a revelation I had recently in therapy: that I wanted—no needed—to find my access to my inner Spain all over again.

A huge part of my life was missing ever since I came home from Barcelona, and I needed to reclaim it. I needed to stop blaming others and external circumstances for my lack of happiness, success or peace, and just surrender it. That café was my sign, and I chose to extend my stay one more night. I did not want to live with the regret of leaving too soon, and it was the right decision to make. We all had an opportunity to strengthen our new friendships even more, and it helped me to alter my state of mind from this emotional turmoil to one of joyous peace within—and take it home with me.

I have been back to California to visit these friends four times since, each trip different, yet never matching the experience of my first time. Some visits were downright disappointing, and eventually the blissful union of souls was no more. Though I remain individually connected to almost everyone I met that first night, the magic of the community is physically gone. But I will never forget the power of our togetherness; of the light and love that was brought into my life; of the intense healing I received that opened me up to more intimate relationships, more powerful ways of being and more love for myself. It was a journey that was divinely created for me, and I will cherish the memories and lessons forever.

27. Bonding Time at Rockin' Horse Ranch

Here is an example of a limiting belief that I was introduced to in my first astrology reading: how can I go on adventures when I have the responsibility of raising two kids on my own? I still remember the answer clear as day: "Take them with you. They signed up for the adventure. They wanted Indiana Jones for a mother. Take them with you."

Part of why I resisted having kids in the first place was because I thought that would mean having to give up traveling. And then as I divorced, and wanted to get back into adventure, some loved ones expressed their concern about me going out on my own so much. But after years of living like a hermit, I just couldn't resign myself to giving up traveling and exploring, yet realistically, my ex didn't take the kids enough for me to go on jaunts that lasted more than four hours at a stretch, and my family was getting maxed out on the babysitting from helping me out with work. It was a big dilemma I was facing, trying to marry the two sides of me as the responsible mom and the need for variety.

So when I heard those words, the biggest lightbulb went off. How on earth did I never think of that before? I mean, no, I couldn't take them with me for a girls weekend in Atlantic City, but I certainly could take them to different places and expose them to exciting new cultural opportunities, unique activities and other out-of-the-house moments. Maybe that would be the best thing for them, to experience life outside of our four walls. My childhood was very

> *I needed to get past this fear about being a single parent.*

home-based, and there was such a security in that, growing up close with our neighbors and having family parties. Yet, I always yearned for something more. What if my kids were the same way? What if they didn't want just the security and shelter of home and neighbors? There was only one way to find out.

I decided on a spring weekend when my daughter had off from school to take them somewhere new. This would be my very first trip alone with them. I had done plenty of day trip adventures with them, both alone and with family members, but I wanted to do something completely different. I needed to get past this fear about being a single parent. I needed to push myself outside of my comfort zone and prove to myself that I was more than capable of taking my children on vacations on my own, and bonding with them as a family unit. I needed to see that being just the three of us was more than okay; it was an adventure itself.

After some research, I decided on taking them to a place upstate, the Rocking Horse Ranch. It was a resort I had gone to for my senior trip in high school, and I remember it being a pretty cool place. They offered a package with a room, meals and amenities, so I thought something all-inclusive that was a distance away, yet not too far away, would be a great first start. We only went for a few days, and it certainly was an experience to remember. They were really excited about the idea of going somewhere on a "vacation," and since they were so used to long car rides, it was a piece of cake to travel to.

When we got there, they were all cute and curious. I told them it was a ranch, and it had horses and cowboy stuff, so the three of us decided that we should all get cowboy hats. After checking into our room, we went down to the souvenir shop and each picked out our own hats to wear and then walked around showing them off. It completely brought out my inner child, and since they were so used to seeing me as a serious mommy (what I thought I had to be), there was pure joy in their faces to see me get all silly and playful with them like this.

The first night we spent just walking around and getting settled into our room. We looked at all of the different things we could do the next day, and then after dinner, we just hung out in our room. That was a bit of an adjustment for them, not being in their own beds. Thankfully, they were two little tiny bodies because the only way anyone was going to get any rest was if the three of us were in the same bed, making a mommy sandwich. Once they felt safe that I was right there with them as they fell asleep, they got comfortable and settled down quickly.

The next day started our exploration. It was a bit misty, with a threat of rain, and the pool was closed, so there were a lot less activities we were able to do than I expected. I didn't consider that much of the outdoor events I thought were included wouldn't be open yet since the weather wasn't warm enough. We played a bit on the playground, and then I took them to go on some pony rides. My daughter was absolutely petrified, and I tried to get her to do it, but forcing her was not the best idea, and I had her taken off after a round. (I had thought that once she got on, she would be okay, but apparently not.) My son was too little at that point to get on, so that idea was a bust.

Luckily, there were some arts and crafts activities going on for us to do, and the kids loved that. They got to paint and make a big mess, and they both ended up making me something, which I still have and treasure today. By this time, the rain had come on full force, so we had to make do with what was inside. We started out with the arcade, but neither one of them were big fans. We walked around the shop and lobby, and it was pretty boring. I remember feeling like this was not going well, and that this wasn't a good idea after all. Our first adventure together was a complete disaster.

Until we discovered there was an indoor "waterpark." I didn't remember seeing anything about that on the website, or being told about it when I got there. So after finding this gem, I asked the front desk about it, and it was included as part of our package. Score! We were going to try it out the next day. I took the kids around to look at it, and they both seemed to light up a bit with excitement. We went to bed to get a good night's rest, and then after a good breakfast in the morning (a quick one—there were too many tugs to come on already to really sit down and enjoy it) we were on our way to see what this indoor water area was all about. Up until then, both my youngin's were squeamish about being around water. They didn't really like to swim, and really didn't like sprinklers. But something intrigued them about this, and there was a perfect little area set up for the smaller children with wade-deep water, a few slides and some squirting sea creatures.

The giggles flowed as much as the water. They jumped, laughed and splashed, and I got in on the action with them. They loved the slides, and trying to run away from the sprays before they got squirted. My previously scared-on-a-pony, avoider-of-pools daughter found her brave side and surprised me by trying out the "big" slide that landed her in a foot of water. She went on it over and over, and my son soon caught on and wanted to go on as well. Before I knew it, my two little munchkins had opened up their inner adventurers and were having a complete blast. They didn't want to leave. We spent the entire day there, save for our meals and dessert. We were going home the next day, but seeing that kind of joy on their faces, I decided that after checkout, I would let them play a little longer and we would just leave later so that they could enjoy the water again.

It felt good to see them so excited over something, with such pure joy, and I received tons of hugs of gratitude for being "the best mommy ever." It was an experience that truly did begin to bond us as a unit of three, and it was extremely healing for me. I accepted the concept of this being my family without my ex-husband; that I could do this on my own; and that adventure can absolutely include my children—and in fact, proved to be an even better adventure than my others because of one simple difference: they brought out my inner child, and I realized that for the first time in a very, very long time, I myself felt safe to play.

28. Into the Woods: Our First Camping Experience

Growing up, there were certain things that just didn't jive with me. Like sports, dirt, bugs and anything medical. I somehow had it ingrained into my head that I was in no way a girl who would enjoy the outdoors, because of said sports, bugs, dirt and could-be injuries. Outdoor activities were never really on my radar, or "to do" list. So, when I was invited by some friends of mine to go camping, I didn't know how to react or respond.

Traditionally, I would have balked at the idea and made some kind of comment about being an indoor girl. But something was different about this invitation: my curiosity. I had finally gotten to a place in my life where I realized being open-minded and taking risks led to some pretty powerful experiences, so I did a double take about this invitation and gave it some thought. Still using the joke that I was an indoor girl, I accepted and actually got excited about doing something so completely out of character. I told the kids what we were going to do, and they seemed excited about it, too.

I remember telling my mom, and her saying, "The kids probably wouldn't like it. You didn't like it when you were little, so I am surprised you are even thinking about it." And that is when it dawned on me; she wasn't using reverse psychology, but that's exactly the a-ha type of moment I had. My response was so automatic, that I didn't even have time to process what I was about to say: "We have never been camping. I can't pretend to know what my kids like and dislike, and just because I don't like something, doesn't mean that I shouldn't let them experience different kinds of adventures so they can find out what they do like. We will never know if we never try." And that was that. From that moment on, I decided this adventure thing was a team decision: we would all be open enough to try new experiences and support each other in them, whether we typically enjoyed them or not.

So, off I went to do research on how to camp. I didn't have even the first clue about it. I camped once when I was a girl scout and hated it (though in fairness, I could attribute that to another trip where I felt left out and without friends, so maybe it wasn't the bugs after all). Thankfully my friend and her family (most of whom I already knew pretty well) knew exactly what to do, and had the basics all figured out. I was able to borrow a tent and many of the supplies I would need, especially since I had no idea if I would ever do this again, and I wasn't about to invest money into all of this just for one weekend. All packed and ready to go, the kids and I headed out to the Hamptons for our second official adventure together as a family—not having the slightest clue what to expect.

Which turned out to be absolutely perfect. It was not what I thought it would be. Such a Virgo, I worried about bathrooms, showers and sanitation, to find that it was all a modern-day set-up that addressed all my hygiene concerns. That in itself, was a game changer. I could relax now knowing I didn't have to suffer with truly "roughing it." I was then able to enjoy the experience a little bit more, seeing that it was a campground, with amenities, and that my friends had an awesome camp and were so helpful in getting me all set up. It was only a few of us together, so I felt like a part of this close-knit family. I was the only "outsider," but I still felt at home with them. Even when I was nervous about my

> *Once the sun set, that is when the sweetest of memories were actually made.*

young son running off, or about the potential tick bites, or what to do, everyone was so kind and helpful towards the single mom out of her element. The kids played nicely together, us women were able to have some nice chats while the men went off and did their thing. The day was spent settling in and just getting to know the area, and the weather was absolutely gorgeous.

Once the sun set, that is when the sweetest of memories were actually made. We sat around a campfire, making and eating s'mores, laughing, joking and just having an absolutely amazing time. My kids were loving every moment of it—and truth be told, so was I. Here I was, in a place that I never in a million dreams ever thought I would be in, and I realized that I actually loved camping. I loved communing with and being in nature. I loved the connections that are created around a campfire. I loved the idea of disconnecting from electricity and computers. It touched my heart in a lot of ways. But mostly, because my children got to experience something completely new, and enjoyed it as well. The only part they hated was having to go to bed.

Bedtime was rough that first night. Our bed kept deflating; there was a hole in it. So I was doing everything I could to keep them comfortable instead of sleeping on the ground, especially my little one. Eventually, I got them to settle down, and I found myself without a bed. Quiet and asleep, I snuck back out to see if the campfire was still lit, and it was. Luckily, there was also a lounge chair waiting there for me to get some rest in—but, as I soon found out, I was not going to be resting quite yet.

Only moments after settling into that lounge chair, one of the guys there I had recently met had come out from his tent and joined me by the fire. It had to be about 1 in the morning; I had thought everyone was asleep. I will never forget that night, ever. The two of us talked for probably hours by that fire. We immediately hit it off; it was as if I knew him forever. And he was so incredibly kind, compassionate and affectionate.

There was a point when I was starting to get cold, and he had moved in closer and held me a bit to warm me up. It was such a sincerely awesome moment, because for a while, we just stayed there, silent by this breathtaking fire, in a slight snuggle. There were no sexual passes made—which you would think would be frustrating, but it wasn't. In fact, it was just the opposite. Here was this man I really connected with, simply holding me, showing affection by merely caring enough to want to keep me warm, and that made this moment such a beautiful one for me.

For so long, I had wished for affectionate love. I crave that love more than any other type. More than the fun flirtations, the passionate sex or even the tense attractions. And while I was in California with my friend, I had realized my need for affection, and less than a year later, here I was being reminded of what I truly wanted to feel. It was actually a quite romantic-like moment by the fireplace, with nothing but a gentle kiss on the forehead goodnight before I fell asleep—and it was so much more profound and meaningful than I could have ever dreamed up.

This connection was exactly what I had needed that night. With a sore, recently rejected heart (unbeknownst to anyone there at that campsite), it's as if he somehow intuitively knew I needed some gentleness in my life at that very moment. And although I have had moments of deep affection in my life since that trip, none have ever matched the compassionate innocence of that fireplace interlude.

Between feeling safe and genuinely cared about by someone I barely knew, and feeling empowered and surprised by how much I enjoyed a trip outside of my adventure box, this camping weekend remains one of the highlights of my travels. I never expected to have such an amazing time, and it just proved to me how wonderful life can be when you just let your guard down—in any way. For me, I had let go of my close-mindedness about the outdoors, and my neediness for false male attention. And what I received in return for it was a true testament to the concept of surrender.

29. My Vegan Thanksgiving in San Diego

When I decided to open my mind up to new opportunities, I really didn't hold back. I went all in. So when the chance arose to take a trip to San Diego to meet a dear friend, I jumped on it. Every other Thanksgiving, I alternate having the kids for the holiday with my ex. When it comes time for them to be with him, I will admit it is a little hard. Although I am so grateful to have the pleasure of spending almost every day of their life with them, and that is a much bigger blessing than celebrating one "designated" special day of the year with them, when it comes time to sit down at the holiday meal, and go to sleep alone in an empty house afterwards, I feel the pangs of missing them.

So one year, I decided that I wanted to do something different. I wanted to change up how I celebrated Thanksgiving, and break away from tradition. Although it was hard on my family for both me and the kids to be missing that year, this trip to San Diego turned out to be divinely timed in many ways. I was already feeling uncomfortable about the prospect of being with the family since I was estranged from one of my cousins and they were considering having individual family holidays to begin with because of it. My leaving actually gave them a huge gift: they all were able to come together for a beautiful family celebration without me, which would unknowingly be their very last Thanksgiving with my cousin. Had the shadow of my presence and family disunity been there, they would not have had that opportunity to enjoy the holiday as much as they did, and for that, I am forever grateful for the universe's orchestration of that event. My cousin needed it, and my family needed that memory to hold on to.

Being away from the kids for a few days can be hard, but it is also very welcomed. Single parenting (<u>any</u> parenting) is not easy, so I do enjoy my chances to go off on my own and take a break. It's just who I am, and it has nothing to do with my kids, who I absolutely cherish and adore. I had never been to San Diego before, and my friend was hosting a Thanksgiving feast where a few other of my friends were invited to join. I didn't tell the other friends, because I wanted to surprise them. I was so excited to see them all again, and couldn't wait to hug them.

But nothing went according to plan; a week before the holiday, there was a huge falling out and none of my other friends could make it down. I was devastated. At the time, I took it personally, and really hard. I was coming out from across the country to see everyone, and they just needed to travel a few hours south— even if not on the holiday itself, in the few days after that when I would still be there. Holidays were supposed to be a time of peace, togetherness and gratitude, and it was starting to feel like anything but.

Luckily, the friend I stayed with is a positive, upbeat kind of person who really can make rainbows out of anything. Although I had this huge disappointment, I was here to spend time with her and was looking forward to expanding my horizons in this vegan household. Arriving on Thanksgiving Day itself, I tormented her a bit in the car by having a turkey sandwich on the way to her house from the airport. (Hey, some traditions I just can't break!) But I spent the rest of the day helping her as best I could to prepare a vegan Thanksgiving meal, which was pretty darn delish! After all,

I came to realize that it wasn't the turkey that made the holiday meal, it was actually all the yummy sides. (Oh yeah, and the company!). Her friends who joined us were absolutely sweet and welcoming, and I felt right at home with them.

Yet at the same time, I felt shy, still a little upset, missing my kids and fighting an allergic reaction to her cats. I was to spend the night at a neighbors house to begin with, so once I got there, I was able to clear my breathing and spend some quiet time reflecting on everything that had happened. It was a very nice—and very different—holiday, and I found myself enjoying breaking a bit of tradition in a search for my own. I declared then that I would spend my "off-years" doing something completely different, because it felt right for me.

The rest of my time in San Diego proved to be pretty powerful. The next day we headed down to the beach. It was absolutely breathtaking. We sat and talked for hours, and I used that time to really pull myself back to center (as I always did whenever I spent time at the beach). So peaceful and warm, once again I felt at home with my feet at the very spot where the ocean meets the sand. There, I asked that the tide take away all that does not serve me in my life, and then wash onto me all of the possibilities for new opportunities to fill that happy, open space.

After my little therapy session with the ocean, I went back and sat down in the sand next to my friend and just started playing around. Next thing I knew, my little sandcastle attempt looked like a shell and I felt like making a turtle. I sculpted a little head, then gave him a tail and some legs, and then I thought he needed eyes and a cute smile. I then felt the impulse to draw a heart on his back. So then I laughed and called him my little love turtle. Slowly, but surely, love was on its way. I also stuck my finger in him and made a circle and wondered why I did that. She said it was an easy button—but later we would come to see its prophetic meaning.

> *My initial instinct was correct; to slow down, to be patient, to allow, to not always be in a rush.*

So after the beach, we decided to go to a Meditation Garden. It was so calm and beautiful, overlooking the ocean. I felt so at peace there. I meditated and received some answers I was looking for, then we headed to the gift shop. I always love to bring back something to remind me of where I've been, and usually it's just some trinket. But this time, I asked my guides to let me find something of great value and meaning to bring back. In less than a minute, my friend came up behind me carrying this little turtle incense holder…and there was the hole, in the same space as I drew it in the sand. You bet I bought it, and it now proudly has become the center of my altar in my bedroom.

I clearly took the turtle as a sign. My initial instinct was correct; to slow down, to be patient, to allow, to not always be in a rush. With the drawing of the heart, I took it to mean have patience about love, for it is on its way and slowly being crafted just for the both of us. But when I read up on the turtle totem, I came to realize not only how much more it meant, but how eerily accurate the message was for me then and how in tune it was with my own heart's warning. To this day, I continue to see my turtles and messages, and have associated the turtle as my official animal totem, which is perfect for someone always trying to live life faster than she needs to.

But that was not the end of the healing to be done on this trip. I also had the honor of receiving a craniosacral session from my friend, who had so much insight to provide about me from simply reading my body. I had ignored the message then, but I was told that my body rejects wheat and dairy, and that I should consider eliminating them from my diet. Although it took me a few months to accept that possibility, I did eventually come to find that in fact, my body does reject those kinds of foods, and the moment I stopped eating them was the moment I shifted my life in many ways—my energy, my health, my weight, even my skin.

To say that I learned a lot on this three-day only trip is an understatement. But it was exactly what I needed. I needed to explore and accept that it was okay for me to break tradition, and that there was a higher reason for it. I needed to experience some disappointment to get over myself, and realize that not everything happens to me on purpose. Sometimes, it has nothing to do with me at all; life just happens and we have to roll with the punches. I needed time for self-reflection, and to get in touch with the message of my totem, and the message of my body. And I needed to do that within the safety of a dear, dear friend who inspires me daily to live life to the fullest with curiosity and openness.

30. A Defining Moment: My Graduation in Miami

Not every trip I have taken was for the intention of pure enjoyment. This particular trip was taken as a great sense of pride and accomplishment. Unbeknownst to anyone but a few select family members and close friends, I was secretly pursuing my masters degree in psychology online in the evenings after work. By keeping it private, it motivated me to successfully keep my work and school responsibilities separate from each other, where one never affected the other. I also felt like I didn't need to announce what I was doing for personal reasons; I needed to prove to myself—and myself alone—what I was capable of, without anyone's approval or disapproval swaying my experience.

And what I found I was capable of was graduating with a full masters in a year and a half with a 4.0, all while holding down a full-time job, being a hands-on single mother, and offering my services as a part-time volunteer for a website community. Tired though I was, I was passionate about it all, and it filled my life with joy. I love school and learning; I always have. And since it was online, everything was written, including long final papers, and crazy as it sounds to others, it was an educational pursuit come true to use my written word over physical participation.

The time came for my graduation, which was to be held in Miami. I had officially graduated in August, but the ceremony was not until January. During this lapse in time, I also enrolled in and became certified as a life coach, so the completion of my education and training coincided with this official graduation.

It was an extremely bittersweet time for me. I was so incredibly proud of myself for what I had accomplished, and the success in which I accomplished it. I was honored to go to Miami to sit among my peers and be called up to receive my official diploma. My family was unable to attend for financial reasons; plus, I couldn't afford to also fly my children down with me, so I had asked my mom to stay behind and watch them, so that I would feel at peace. There was going to be a live online viewing of the event, so although it was not the same as being there in person, it gave me and my family some comfort to know that they would absolutely be there in some way, even if in spirit.

I wasn't disappointed in that, really. I understood completely, and this was more of something I needed to do for myself rather than for others. I knew I had the love and support back home, rooting me on. My children were busy making me presents for when I returned, along with planning a little surprise party for me. And when I came home, I did have all that love, joy and pride of my family and friends who recognized me and made my graduation time really special.

The only time it felt a little sad was when I walked across the stage to get my diploma, with my name called out, knowing there was no one in the audience genuinely clapping for me, or waiting to give me a hug. However, there was another girl I had befriended who generously shared her family with me, who were more than happy to give me hugs of pride and congratulate me in the moment.

But the feeling of immense joy made all of it worth it. I had done this. I had sacrificed long nights reading, writing and studying

> *I was no longer just a mom, or just an employee. I was my own woman, following my dreams, and making them happen.*

to earn top grades and graduate with honors. Divorce did not bring me down, but instead, inspired me to take on this risk. It never affected my job, or my time with my children, but it gave me a true sense of identity. I was no longer just a mom, or just an employee—I was my own woman, following my dreams, and making them happen. This was for me, and although I do not need a piece of paper to prove my worth, it certainly made me feel special and accomplished. I just needed to have faith in myself.

As magical as this moment was for me, there were also other situations going on in my life that made this a less than stellar moment for me. I had just come home from another trip out to Los Angeles the week before, where I was able to meet even more of the amazing connections I had made online at a special anniversary party. That was a wonderful part of the trip, where friendships were deepened and new memories were made.

But not everything was as warm and fuzzy as the times before, and relationship breakdowns were happening, and trusts were being broken. I was questioning who my friends truly were, and why I was exerting so much energy into people and activities that didn't seem to be investing back in me. On top of all of that turmoil was another turn of events that put a bit of a damper on my trip to Miami, which ended in not being able to meet up with a new friend of mine I still believe I am destined to meet one day.

Yes, my purpose down there was to receive my diploma with pride, which I did. But sitting at a Cuban café, and sitting alone on the beach the day before was not how I had envisioned this trip. The vibe of relationship breakdowns everywhere was not what I envisioned during that whole month. Two trips gone wrong, which should have been such utter highlights of my life. I guess in a sense they were; they highlighted the character of who I was being during that time, and the hypocrisy of expectations I held of others versus the standards I bent for myself and my own behavior. It made me take a good, hard look at who I had become.

Yes, I was a successful business woman, with a new degree, certification and additional wisdom in metaphysical subjects. But what I also was, was a mom who spent a little too much time socializing, flirting and avoiding sitting still in an attempt to block out the pain and seek the attention that I thought I was denied throughout my marriage (and my childhood). It was an awakening that I was seeking way too much external validation and hope to get me through some trying years. And it was the culmination of these two trips that led me to truly accept the healing I had ahead of me: to find my self-worth, my self-respect and my self-love. And to recognize that all that was happening was a necessary breakdown to lead me within.

31. What Happens in AC, Doesn't Always Stay There (Part 2)

I am way too far away from Vegas to get into that intensity of trouble; but the proximity of Atlantic City has served its purpose in my life. Unless I am traveling with a spouse or parent, or for business, trips to AC were always quite memorable. I can't get into all of them in this book; so I only offer up the most eventful and insightful ones.

This particular trip was with a good friend of mine from work. Work had been very stressful and busy, so when the time came for us to have a weekend getaway to Atlantic City, we were more than ready for the break. All we wanted was to do some gambling, a little dancing and spend some time on the beach. Nothing too crazy, but definitely fun. After my last trip debacle, I was looking forward to a non-drama weekend with a dear friend. Oh Jenny, don't you know by now that this sometimes is just not possible?

Things started out normal, with our check-in and doing some basic gambling before getting ready for a night out. Then we had an amazing Cuban dinner and some drinks at a yummy restaurant while we tried to figure out where we wanted to spend the evening. We had settled on visiting Harrah's, where there was an indoor pool nightclub that was supposed to be off the hook. All of our plans were set for a pretty normal evening, and then the craziest coincidence walked up. One of her exes and good friend happened to be at the same exact hotel as us for the weekend, and they decided to meet us up at Harrah's later that night. Her and her ex did not part on the greatest of terms, but enough time had gone by where it was civil, and even an opportunity for them to find peace. So we agreed to let them tag along on our adventure.

Now let me tell you about this friend, the player. He didn't know that I knew he was already seeing a mutual friend of ours. (Can we say small world?) So the flirtation with me began. And then we arrived at the club, and I watched him work the two levels to find himself a woman that night. My friend and I went on to do our own thing, including dancing in the pool and having a complete blast. Things then got boring (and the player couldn't find someone to take home), so we all decided to leave and find somewhere else to go. We ended up back at our own hotel, where the guys graciously paid for our covers into another dance club.

We were dancing, letting loose and just having an absolute great time. My girlfriend and I loved to dance, and were surprised when the guys started dragging us out to go. I thought it was because they didn't like the music (though they were dancing), but turns out, as we exited and I asked what the problem was, player admitted that although it was fun, he'd rather spend some alone time with me. A-ha. So transparent. But we played along, and decided to head up to their room for some beer and chatting. We had fun, from singing and dancing in the elevator on the way up, to mock professional wrestling in the room. The four of us really did get along well, so we had a great time.

But then the awkwardness started. It took a great deal of (internal) strength to stop anything from happening with this boy. I couldn't go there. Not that he wasn't attractive and charming. Not that I wasn't feeling it. But he was dating a friend of mine. I couldn't do that to my friend, but that was really just a convenient excuse that actually was empowering me to follow through on my "no thank you." I needed to say no for me. Because for the first time in my life, I was choosing self-worth over attention, self-respect over meaningless sex and self-love over ego.

He certainly didn't make it easy. I had to pull out all of the stops. I pretended to be in the bathroom puking from "drinking too much" so that he would think I was sick. You would think that would be a turn off, but Mr. Persistent was still trying. I had even excused myself to my room (after pulling my friend on the side and letting her in on what I was doing) to end the opportunity once and for all, but when they went back out for a little bit, he apparently grabbed her phone, found my number and called me. Of course I answered thinking it was my friend, but it was him, and I had to turn him down again.

I didn't like the feeling of rejecting this other person, who was making me feel really desirable—something I don't get a lot. But when I say I went to sleep with so much respect and pride for myself, it was like I was a whole new person. In that moment, all those discoveries I've had about men came rushing back to me, along with a few more. I wasn't going to be with a man who a friend claimed exclusivity with. I didn't need to prove to myself I was attractive by engaging with what would have been two men during the same time period.

I woke up the next day feeling good. I didn't have a single regret about turning him down, and my heart felt light and happy over my decision. My ego does go back there from time to time and wonder what things could have been like if I had chosen differently, but my heart already knows that answer: it would have set in motion a pattern of guilt, self-degradation and unnecessary turmoil for what most likely would have been 5 minutes of enjoyment. And although I haven't always made the best choices in love since that time, it did help to clear up a few patterns and beliefs that were no longer working for me, and were in fact blocking me from heart healing.

I walked away feeling good that I honored a friendship and honored myself. It being the last day of our trip, we spent the rest of our time there getting massages, relaxing on the beach and avoiding the awkwardness of the morning after that never was.

32. Disney Cruising with the Family

After a bunch of intense, purposeful, healing-driven travel stories, it feels so good to sit back and reflect on a much more joyous and carefree experience. I guess that's because of all of the work I had put in, and all of those side journeys that were important for teaching me lessons and bringing me back to my core. This one was just about being myself, connecting with my family and just having a genuinely good time.

I love to travel to Disney in between holidays; first, because it is the slowest time of year there, and second, because they have a lot of magical holiday events that really get you into the spirit. I had convinced my mother and sisters (with very little arm twisting, mind you) to join me and the kids on a Disney cruise. We would spend a day at the resort and parks before embarking on a 4-night cruise, and they were all down for the new experience. I was the only one who ever had the cruise experience before, and like last time, I was excited for them to share in my joy.

This time was different. I chose to be more laid back and open to others' travel preferences, and at the same time, the years had brought a maturity and closeness for all of us that guaranteed this trip would not be like the last time. Early in the morning we were set for our flight out; my son's first, my daughter's second (though she didn't remember her last one) and a terrified mother who, thankfully, kept it all in so that the kids didn't feed off of her fear of flying and develop a sense of their own. Neither child had

> *I am there to experience the experience; not to worry about what is going on somewhere else.*

an issue and actually loved flying. Their enthusiasm trickled over to my mom, which helped to alleviate her own anxiety a bit—or at the very least, distract her.

We got to the hotel, and the excitement really began. The kids were in awe, as was my family, to see a Christmas tree in the lobby, and then the adorable character-themed towel folding welcome on our guest room beds. We stayed at the All-Star Movies resort, so the theme was lighthearted and fun, and less grown up, which brought out everyone's playful side. We settled in for a bit and grabbed some lunch before setting off for our first adventure: Magic Kingdom.

Since it was off-season, it was less crowded. We went on the traditional rides, and the kids were just so in awe of everything (including mommy's special tiki room dancing and singing). There were some rides they weren't impressed with, but as my sisters ironically tried to teach them, they had to be open to enjoying what everyone else loved to do because that was what family vacations were all about. Gratefully, my kids were young enough to grasp that concept a lot more easily than my then-teenage sisters did. Knowing how special this trip was to all of us, with it being my first "real" vacation with the kids since the divorce, and the first real one with my own immediate family (minus my dad) since the last Disney trip, I had some surprises up my sleeve.

I had the kids get into their Cinderella and Prince Charming costumes, and then led everyone to Cinderella's castle. Not understanding why the kids had to be dressed up, or why we were actually entering inside the castle, they soon caught on that we were about to have a special Princess lunch in the castle. Everyone was so excited, especially the kids. They got to talk to all of the princesses, and even my son blushed a bit as he posed with some of his favorites as our only prince. The food was delicious, and the whole dining experience was magical. It definitely was a meal to remember. To add to the magic, I had purchased tickets for us to stay on into the evening hours for a special after-hour Christmas in the park event, with extra riding time, specialty shows and a whole bunch of other holiday touches, including fireworks. Unfortunately, we were all a bit too tired to truly enjoy the evening for long, and headed back to retire, but the day in the park proved to be a very good start to our family vacation.

The cruise was an equally great time. From the delicious meals, to the captivating shows, to the port adventures, we all enjoyed ourselves. Well, except for the first part of the trip where one of my sisters was very ill from seasickness and ended up in the boat's emergency room. But she was a trooper—nothing was stopping her from having fun. The first night was rough for all of us, but as we started to get our sea legs, the rest of the trip went swimmingly.

Everyone found something they loved. We all loved the deck parties, fireworks, off-shore beach day and barbecue and holiday events, like the Christmas tree lighting. The kids loved the pools and sprinkler areas and the unlimited ice cream on the boat, and got a kick out of alternating being on the top bunk bed. And they would giggle with fits of laughter at seeing the different animal towel creations that awaited us in the room. My daughter especially looked forward to the shows at night. My son really loved going out on our balcony in the morning to see the sun come up, and enjoyed swimming in the ocean with me. He just wasn't a big fan of taking pictures with the characters, and made a grumpy face each time. And my daughter was freaked out about the fish in the water at the beach, so it was kinda cute to see her flip out and refuse to swim. She kept my mom company as she relaxed on the beach—something my mom rarely does, but you could tell she enjoyed immensely.

My mom also loved the shops and all of the little activities going on around the boat. My sisters enjoyed swimming with the dolphins and the night life, and trying new foods with me at dinnertime. Me? I enjoyed it all, plus an amazing massage and quiet time in the adults only pool area for a spell—but mostly, I enjoyed the fact that I could not have a cell phone on, and no one could reach me for anything.

I was absolutely free. Everyone I needed to be in contact with was with me. I didn't have to worry about checking my phone or emails; I left it all behind. It made me more present to who I was with, and what I was doing, and I think that single-handedly was the reason we all were able to truly enjoy ourselves and each other. All we had was each other, and that was all we needed. When we needed to go off on our own, we did. When we wanted to do something together, we were all on board. At times, I needed to do things alone with the kids, and at times, I needed some me time while they had the chance to spend quality time with the kids without me. It was such an easy-going, non-itinerary driven kind of vacation, yet we still all got to experience everything we wanted to.

There was no fighting. There was peace, and appreciation, and pure enjoyment about spending time together. The only time normal life tension occurred was when we were first checking in, and as we waited in the airport to board the plane to go home. Oh, did I mention that was because the phones were turned back on and we had all forgotten how to stay present in the moment?

Although for me, since that trip, I do make a concerted effort myself that any trip I take, my phone is completely off. If I am with the kids, I allow myself a courtesy call or text to my mom just to touch base, but that is it. When I do not have my kids, I turn my phone on only once per day to call them to say good night. If there is an emergency, people know where I can be found, but I have faith that everything will be okay, so there is no need for me to keep a phone by my side just in case.

I am there to experience the experience; not to worry about what is going on somewhere else. And that one small change has had a ripple effect not only in my most adventuresome adventures, but also in my local outings and quality time spent with loved ones. It has made all the difference in how I connect and enjoy the time that I have with them, or to myself—and that is the only profound lesson that came out of this particular trip, except for the reminder of how much I truly and deeply love my family, and wish for many more moments just like these.

33. Home is Where the Heart Heals: A NYC Experience

Readers would not know this, but I went out of order in writing this chapter on purpose because in this moment, it is cathartic for me to do so. We all go through periods of healing, and have relationships that challenge us to be better, stronger, wiser and more true to ourselves. These relationships are healers in and of themselves, as what we deny about ourselves is the truth of their mirror. The faults of others, and blaming the failure of friendships and relationships on others, is merely us being in denial of how we are the exact same way. Perhaps we do not demonstrate it in the same way. And this is not meaning that someone else's actions are not harmful, hurtful or even unintentional; but it is a calling to see where we are letting ourselves—and others who cherish us—down.

Which brings me to how apropos writing this chapter is in this moment, as the experience for me has just come full circle. What began as a curiosity about yet another healing technique completely transformed my entire life. And I know people say that all the time, and I know I have alluded to intense experiences that affected me profoundly throughout this book. But this one truly led to multiple levels of awareness, healing and transcendentalism in many areas of my life. Sometimes the deepest revelations come from your own backyard; literally, and figuratively.

For me, this experience opened up many doors: forgiveness, compassion, true intimacy and a keen sense of why we need to live in the present, and not the past or the future. I attended a weekend seminar that really made me take a hard look at my life, and how everyone else was to blame for life circumstances—except me, of course. I had to own my shit (excuse the language) because there was no mercy in this seminar. No, oh you poor thing, of course you are the way you are, it's because XYZ happened to you. There was no understanding; no excuses; no blaming; no outside transference of our internal state of affairs accepted. We literally had to look in the mirror and see that it was our responses, our stories and our refusal to move passed the past that locked us up. Only we have the key to open it up.

You got out of this seminar as much as you were willing to put into it. You had the choice. Talk or take action. Me? I surprised myself by taking action. After 12 years of refusing to speak to him for leaving us and resenting him for having more love for a beer bottle than he had for me, I called my father out of the blue to reconnect with him. I gave him my forgiveness, and asked for his forgiveness in return. For I had realized that I had abandoned him as much as he had abandoned me, and his sickness had no reflection upon his love for me. It was exactly that—a sickness—and it was time to repair the damage and move forward.

I have never felt so peaceful in my entire life, to give up that never-ending story of how he didn't love me because he loved alcohol more. Once I gave that up, I started building a relationship again with him, and I can actually see the love and emotion that was always there, just not in my perfectly created vision of expectation. He loved me on his terms, in his own way, and expresses it differently that I ever could or would, but that shouldn't matter. It no longer matters. I can finally look past my judgments to feel the love that is truly there, and believe in it. I cannot even begin to describe the immense amount of freedom that accompanied this profound childhood forgiveness.

> *I just never counted on death to take that opportunity away from me.*

He even came down shortly after my phone call to visit, and to finally meet the grandchildren I had been denying him. It was pure joy to see the love for them in his eyes, and theirs in return. They loved him, and I was so spiteful in keeping the one thing he always dreamed of away from him: a son (in the form of a grandson). And to witness that bond, not just for his sake, but also for my son's, really showed me that the power of love is so much stronger than the power of anger, fear, revenge or hate. And this newfound relationship with my father began a spiral effect upwards in my life of repairing the relationships I had that needed some work, and opening myself up to new ones.

Over the course of that weekend, I had also made peace with my ex-husband, and took ownership for my role in the destruction of our marriage. I could no longer make him take the full blame for what transpired, even though I found some of his actions to be irresponsible and hurtful at times. He is my mirror: so were mine, just in different ways. We reached a new level of understanding that day, and although we still have our issues, as any couple—together or apart—do, it is easier for us to work through them because that underlying co-hatred was dissolved, and we now can work from a place of forgiveness and peace.

I also had a heart to heart with my mother about some of the events that had transpired over the years between us, and I was surprised at how well the conversation went, and how good it felt to reconnect with my mother again. Even though she had always been there, years of tension caused a rift that we were now ready to repair.

I began a quest to restore my closest relationships that had taken a hit throughout my life, whether due to misunderstandings, jealously, power struggles or simply my cold, hardened interior and wall blocking out the love and genuine care others had to give. I spoke with my sisters, a co-worker at work who I had been especially (and unnecessarily) harsh to and a few friends who had tried to be there for me, but I had convinced myself they really didn't care, just like all the others before. I laid it all out on the table, and life was improving across the board.

There were still a few relationships that actually needed my immediate attention, but I just couldn't find the courage to deal with them. I was too busy being self-righteous and trying to find a way to communicate how I felt. I wanted to make peace, but not invite certain situations back into my life—I just didn't know how to handle it, so I let it go with the thought that when the time is right, I will deal with it.

I just never counted on death to take that opportunity away from me. With one shocking phone call, I was rocked to my core: my cousin had unexpectedly passed. My family was now facing an unspeakable tragedy, and reality hit hard that day. I had made peace with my father, knowing I did not want him to pass without us healing things, and never saying what we've always wanted to say. And then it happens with my cousin. The guilt was all-consuming.

Not only that, but I had to face members of my family who I had been somewhat distanced from because of my estrangement with my cousin; a family I feared was now torn apart forever because of it. My cousin had died; I had rejected him in life, and I was afraid they would reject me now, and ban me from being there for his death. The wait was torture; I could not call to offer my condolences. How do you tell a grieving family you are sorry for everything, when you can't even take anything back? It was too late now. Or so I thought.

My cousin (with the help of divine powers) had better plans for all of us. I went over to see my aunt and uncle, anxious about the possible anger they had towards me. But instead, my aunt opened her arms and hugged me. She said my cousin always knew and accepted my distance, and never blamed me for how I felt. He had understood, and had told them that over and over, and they felt like they had to respect that; if he knew in his heart it was okay, they had to be okay, too. So the tragedy that could have torn us all apart, actually ended up drawing us closer together.

I still have pangs of guilt from time to time about not physically working it out with my cousin, but I do talk to him now, and can feel his forgiveness and understanding. But it sure taught me a great lesson—you really can't expect tomorrow to come to say the words you need to say, to express or ask for forgiveness, or to show compassion to those that need it the most, even if you are angry or not aligned with them. It was an extremely tough lesson to learn, but an extremely important one. And I am filled with gratitude daily for the graciousness and forgiveness my family showed to me during this time, accepting that my grief was real, and that my heart was just as broken as theirs over this tragedy.

As if all of these conversations and experiences during only a three-month period weren't intense enough, during this time, I also became involved in an unconventional relationship that tested my boundaries—well, pushed them actually, but mostly in a good way. It broke down many walls of fear that I had built up as a result of my childhood and marital experiences, and it taught me profound vulnerability. I learned the true value of allowing intimacy on every level, and the powerful experience of letting someone in to your most sacred of spaces, and feeling safe to do so.

This relationship taught me pain, but it also taught me passion. It brought me down to the lowest feelings of unworthiness at times to recognize the depth of self-worth that I had, recognizing that it was only my self-judgment that made it so. It challenged my beliefs to strengthen them. It gave me courage, support and a sense of unstoppability in going after what I wanted in life, helping me to see who I am at my core, and the amazing person that I truly am. If was definitely life-changing, and I wouldn't give up any moment of it for anything. It was exactly everything I needed to experience at the time, and I have so much love and gratitude for the blessing that it was.

In heartbreak, I found self-love. In showing vulnerability, I found acceptance and surrender. In communicating honestly and openly, no matter how difficult, I found release and peace. For all of its many downsides on the surface, and the ego-responses and stories created about this relationship, there were just as many upsides and karmic healings that needed to take place for the both of us throughout our journey together. And it was a very special one that has left a significant imprint on my life, and in my heart.

Our season is over, but the lessons are not. Everything that has happened as the result of opening up during this seminar continues to bring me to greater awareness, better connections and deepened self-love. A whirlwind of intense, unexpected healing was upon me, and I could choose to walk away, or do the work and fight for my life. I didn't have to go far to find everything I was looking for, to feel whole and complete. I didn't even have to go to this seminar in New York City, or my actual backyard. I just had to go within. And this repeating lesson was finally starting to click with me.

34. Up, Up and Away... In a Hot Air Balloon

For my 30th birthday, my sisters had presented me with a hot air balloon ride, to be taken whenever the three of us were able to find the time to get together. It shouldn't have been too difficult, since we all lived close by and my mom was available to watch my daughter while we went. But life had other plans; I ended up moving to Pennsylvania, with rare trips to New York on the weekends. They had been moving from place to place until they found the right one, and the same experience with jobs and relationships. I had distanced myself, and then after I came back home for good, I was slowly trying to find my grounding. Every time we would try to plan it, it was always right after the perfect season, and by then it was too windy and we'd have to wait another year. This went on for 8 years.

Finally, the three of us said enough is enough, it is time to book the ride and just do it. So there I am, getting ready to finally go on the hot air balloon ride I have been waiting for, and all of these emotions come flooding over me. It was a bit nerve-wracking to see how it actually worked. I think somehow in my mind I pictured a simple hop in and fly up together, but the reality was a little different, as I saw I actually had to climb into the basket and hope it didn't tip over. Now the funniest part is that fear never entered the equation before that point, yet my two daredevil sisters were a bit trepidatious about the whole thing from the start. They had both been bungee jumping before and took other adventurous risks, and seeing them so nervous about it made me wonder: what am I missing?

We get there, and we are told that there is a pretty good chance that we won't go up because the winds are much stronger than predicted. Panic ensues for some, especially those who drove 5 hours to get there. That's a long way to travel for something you paid a lot of money for, and then be told to go back home, possibly for another year, because it was late in the season. We only drove 2.5 hours and just had a kick-ass dinner, so we were not stressing if it was cancelled; though after 8 years, we had waited long enough! They didn't think the winds would actually cooperate, but that's when I entered manifestation mode and talked the wind down—from 10 to 6mph in 10 minutes. Not bad, eh?

Getting the clearance we needed, we all get ready to go on this amazing ride, and I am cool and calm about the prospect of flying up high in the air with no harness and no steering wheel, unpredictability abound. It was very strange to begin with for me, who likes security. But then we are instructed to quickly get into the basket and there is where I freeze and freak—I was worried about the basket tipping over on the ground. Yes, the ground. And people falling on me or me on them—not potentially plummeting to my death from high up in the sky. THIS is what I freak out about—and more so when we were about to hit the ground upon landing. My sister thought my reaction was so priceless, she shot some hopefully never to been seen footage of my fear of falling out of a basket and onto the ground. Great blackmail stuff.

But once I was up in that air and convinced myself that the basket wouldn't tip us over and pour us out like a teacup, it was such an extraordinary experience and it catapulted me into a state of inner peace. Because in that moment, as I floated above the

> *It was like the chains of my reality, my thinking, my beliefs, were all lifted away with the balloon.*

Earth, carried aimlessly by the wind and looking out upon the horizon on one side to see the setting sun and the other to see the light of the almost full moon, it hit me how perfectly representative that experience was of my heart's desires.

To be free without reigns. To soar without knowing the destination, only admiring the journey. To experience ups and downs knowing each movement was completely perfect. To take a risk and relish in the reward. To share that experience with those I love the most. To see the world from an entirely different viewpoint. To be so much more aware of my moment—the barking dogs in the distance, a sense of the friendliness of onlookers as we passed over and waved, the smells of the onions growing on the farm (without tearing!), to literally touch the top of a tree and corn husk in the field—just to take in every bit of it all, and truly appreciate its majesty.

It's what I wished my life to be from that moment on. Living in freedom, taking chances, opening my mind outside of the box, enjoying every single step of the way and sharing my life and experiences with others. It was like the chains of my reality, my thinking, my beliefs were all lifted away with the balloon, and the peace that remained was one that I will hold onto for the rest of my life.

And also to get that start-ups and landings can be shaky—and even scary and risky—but once you start flying on your path, you simply soar. I can't let the fear of being tipped over stop me from the journey. I need to fight through the urge to back off, and just see it through. And remember that there will be people I love right beside me as I confront my fears—just as I am there to help them confront theirs when that time comes. We all have a different battle inside of us, but when we come together in support and love, our breakthroughs can be something truly astounding. Realizing that was a beautiful moment for me.

It's always good to experience something that is a reflection of a journey in your life. Taking this simple hot air balloon ride was one such experience that directly spoke to who I can be in pursuing my dreams, and it opened up such possibilities for me afterwards. It is one of those adventures that can really put life in a new perspective, and when you let go, you can see so much beauty in life from a big picture point of view—rather than limiting ourselves to seeing that what is right in front of us every day is all that there is to it.

35. Life in the Afterglow: A Sedona Awakening

When I first decided to go to Sedona for a meditative retreat hosted by a good friend of mine, something deep within knew it would be a very important event—but I had no idea how truly profound and life-changing it would be. Here I was, in one of the most spiritual places on the entire planet, with access to vortexes, healing energy and lightworkers, and I knew it was a calling to go deep within and allow the transformational experience to unfold. I went with an open heart, open mind and courage to change my life. And change my life, it did.

I was challenged on every possible level: physically, emotionally, mentally, spiritually, socially. I learned surrender; I allowed faith; and I accepted truth.

I had never been hiking before in my entire life, and I did the research, got my hiking boots, took the advice of getting a walking stick and exercised a little each day in the weeks leading up to the trip so that I wasn't completely overwhelmed. I was ready for exhaustion, dehydration—and I will admit it—defeat. I was ready to accept that I would not make it to the top, but that doing my best was all that counted. But the morning before the hike, I shifted that negativity. I called upon angels, something I rarely did, to guide me up the mountain; to help me to see it through to completion and to fight through any challenge, because dammit, this was a lifetime opportunity and I was not going to be a quitter. And I have to say, changing that mindset changed the entire experience.

Butterfly Travels

I barely struggled (thanks to my nifty little walking stick and double bottles of water). There were some rough patches, but I fought through them. And as we got to the top, the terrain was tougher, the rocks bigger and the incline steeper. I was so close, and there was no way I was stopping. So many epiphanies occurred along the way, one of which was my turtle totem reminder that "slow and steady wins the race." I let go of the attachment that I had to keep up with everyone else. This was MY journey, and it became so clear how it was a metaphor for my life journey; my constant pushing forward in a rush, wondering am I there yet? And missing the beautiful opportunities to stop and smell, see, taste, hear, touch the detours. So I stopped when I needed to, and broke away from others when I needed to, and I made it to the top.

Now you would think that was it—the accomplishment of reaching the top! But oh no—my fearless friend had another plan in mind (and true to nature, I let him know exactly what I thought of his crazy little plan). He wanted to go up even higher, across a path a little more dangerous to get to—a place even more breathtaking in the vortex. I resisted—I resisted with every fear, doubt and worry in my entire body. I felt the tears well up inside me, and struggled with my decision as I looked at the unprotected slope. And then courage started building up in me, and I heard the whispers "you can do this, you are safe." So I took my time, looked fear in the face and took a risk that paid off beautifully.

I was on top of the Boyton Canyon, overlooking the beauty of Sedona, and that took my breath away. We enjoyed a beautiful meditation as the sun beat down on us with its blessing, and the winds played with our hair in symphony. How proud I was of myself for pushing past what I only thought were my limits. How safe I have been playing life all of this time.

But that was not the end of my battle. I knew in my heart the whole time that going back down would be my greatest challenge—and it was. But it was also my greatest triumph. I suck at receiving, at asking for help, at allowing vulnerability. But as I was ready to descend, full of fear and anxiety of falling to my death and leaving my children motherless, I drew strength from the people around me. Hands reached out—literally—to walk me down difficult passages. Strangers cleared paths and braced themselves to guide me safely down. I let humor and wit take over as I allowed the most raw, vulnerable part of me to be exposed, and to graciously accept help.

I didn't even think about it. I didn't feel guilty that others were committed to helping me. I didn't feel ashamed that I was really, really scared and needed someone braver than me to rely on. And I cannot tell you how deeply that moment changed me, and the gratitude I felt for all of those loving people. It was such a blessing to feel that deep sense of love and compassion from others who genuinely cared about my well-being. An intimate moment I will never forget.

Once I passed that challenge, I felt like I could fly. I faced fear, I faced potential failure, I faced risk—and I survived in every sense of the word. Although the rest of the travel back down was not without its challenges, there was nothing I couldn't face. A little dehydration, frustration and exhaustion started to creep in, but with the bond of a new friend, and taking the care to listen to my own body cues, we made it through. I learned so much from that one experience—and it set the tone for the rest of the retreat.

So there was my physical and spiritual challenge—pushing my body, and having faith in myself, others and God. I then faced some hardcore emotional challenges when I went for an energy intelligence massage at the spa, and that was no easy session.

> *I faced fear, I faced potential failure, I faced risk—and I survived in every sense of the word.*

Sure, the place was beautiful, the scents of lotions lovely and the heart of the healer kind. But that was some of the hardest work I have ever done to heal myself, and I put every ounce of energy into what felt like a 10-year therapy session.

Deep, deep rooted issues came to the surface, and I had to face my darkest enemy: myself. Not my childhood issues with a parent; not a wound from a bully at school or a broken heart from a past relationship. I came face to face with me. My judgments, my anger, my frustration, my lack of faith, my self abuse—all of it. I was made to sit back and forth between two chairs facing my two selves: responsible, serious, somber Jenny, and happy, adventurous, playful Jenny. And it was painful to watch the two of them go back and forth in disharmony—but I have to say, this was the most brilliant technique for self healing I have ever experienced in my life. By the end of the session, I had found peace between the two sides of me, and joined them together. And from that point on, I felt the change in me. A heaviness lifted, a love restored. And an openness to all that is that I have shut out for way too long.

And by the way—did I mention that was only ONE day? Whew! I was exhausted. But then I was also energized by this new state of being that I had become. It made my mental and social challenges feel like a breeze, because I just became myself with no excuses, judgments or desire for approval. I was able to enjoy the presentations of the retreat leaders on a much deeper level. Usually I would go in with the perspective, "I know most of this" but instead I stayed wide open to hear all of the new possibilities to expand my mind and belief system. I found them fascinating—and I also found new information and alternative concepts I never heard come flowing in to my awareness from my conversations with others at the retreat, fueling my love for learning with excitement. I love, love, love being intellectually stimulated and learning new things, and welcomed a thirst for knowledge that I would take home with me.

I think what amazed me most about this whole experience was the level of comfort I felt around complete strangers. I am surrounded by people I have never met before (in this life), and yet I felt safe and open, like I can say or do anything without a care. Though I still needed a few prickly pear lemonade vodkas to loosen me up to dance in front of others—but hey, I didn't say everything was completely cured (*wink*). We are always a work in progress.

What I did realize in this space was that my radar was activated, affirming my intuition about people—not from a place of judgment, but from a place of understanding and honoring boundaries. I need to trust myself, and release my attachment to wanting approval from others who don't nurture my soul back. It was from this experience that I also had a revelation about the relationships in my life on a grander scale.

I will admit I got the excited goosebumps when someone "recognized" me from my *Confessions* show, or elsewhere. It was pretty cool—but it also didn't give me the fulfillment I thought it would. It gave me gratitude and appreciation for the compliment, and a sense of making a difference in others, but it also left me realizing that it's not what is important. It's not about the viewers, it's about those who genuinely support me and are there by my side. I need to embrace them, and nurture my relationships with those closest to me instead of juggling acquaintances—as lovely and special as they are themselves.

I came home feeling as close as ever to my dear friend who took this adventure with me, and realizing how blessed I am with quite a few true friendships like hers—and how I need to pay more attention to them and make the time to spend with people I love. I already started by connecting better with my children, and letting them be to make their own decisions and mistakes—something else I had an a-ha moment about. Trying to control the people that I love out of my intense love for them and wanting what is best, instead of just allowing them to be, in their path, to grow as they were meant to, blossoming outside of my well-intentioned expectations and advice. And I have already seen the difference in what that shift has made—I empowered my children, and what a beautiful site to watch them grow instead of watch them "behave."

I have no doubt I got more out of this trip than I even imagined. I have made decisions that are aligned with my own integrity and value system—decisions that previously left me afraid of being alone or rejected. I have taken on a more surrendered state of consciousness, working in the flow of challenges instead of stressing against them, and seeing the magic of allowance take away the obstacle. I have called on my angels every day to help me, and allowed them to pull through without my resistance or interference. I feel connected to others in a genuine way. I feel empowered and courageous. I have faith in my God and his love for me. And thanks to the blessed experience under the pristine stars of Sedona, I have an abundance of love for myself. And that, my friends, was the biggest conquest of all.

36. The Renaissance Faire: Unleashing My Inner Princess

After years of always wanting to go to a Renaissance Faire, my wish finally came true. It couldn't have come at a better time, either. It was the day after my birthday, and the week leading up to it was an extremely challenging one. I was faced with several health issues being uncovered, excessive fatigue and emotional heartache. I was feeling a lot of different energies this particular birthday week. I was reflecting on my life, frustrated with the lack of progress in my career, in my financial freedom, in my co-parenting situation, in my friendships that were being put to the test, and the cherry on top, lack of a genuine love life. Cue a birthday full of tears, pity partying and complete isolation.

Luckily for me, I have fantastic friends who pulled me out of this long enough to go out that night and let it all go. Friends who — after much persuasion and insistence — finally got me into my inner child, and onto the dance floor. I felt safe, free and loved in that moment, and nothing else seemed to matter anymore. I came out of my altered state of sad consciousness to realize that all the love I need is all around me, in the form of beautiful children, a supportive family and open-hearted friends.

Why this backstory when this is supposed to be about a Renaissance Faire? It set the stage for my emotional clearing so that I could be open to enjoy the day. Otherwise, I would have brought depression, crankiness and exhaustion into the equation and made everyone else miserable. But instead, the dancing lead me into the heart of my inner child, and from there, the Jenny within was ready to play.

Of course I can't participate in an experience like this without going all the way! Before the festival, we had ordered costumes so that my daughter and I could be fair maidens, and my son could be a knight. I had so much fun getting into that costume that it just lit me up completely. And since I was in such a state of imaginative bliss, I was easygoing and childlike all day. Usually, I am so concerned with itineraries, how my kids felt, how the rest of my companions were, is everyone happy, etc., and for the most part, I was in complete surrender.

We get to the faire and after getting in costume, I spotted a vendor selling floral crowns and like a little child, I jumped up and down with excitement, exclaiming how I wanted one. Apparently, the joy on my face was contagious, as my Godmother, who was with me, asked me if I wanted her to buy me one for my birthday. And in turn, I activated her inner child, as she ended up getting her own green feathered crown of loveliness. I knew right then and there, that this was going to be a very good day. We were ready to be medieval princesses!

But it wasn't going to be without some challenges, as my pre-teen daughter started to cop an attitude of "get me out of the dress" and "this is boring." Being in such a peaceful, blissful state of mind, I didn't really fight with her, surprisingly enough. I told her after a few pictures she can take the costume off and just be comfortable, so she was happy with that compromise. My son chose to stay in his knight costume for most of the day, feeling pretty badass himself, especially after getting a sword.

The first part of the day was a bit of a struggle getting my daughter to relax and enjoy herself. The rest of my family tried to get through to her as well, trying to find something—anything—that she would like there. It was getting a bit frustrating but I decided to just let her be, and not let it ruin my experience. I loved exploring all of the little shops, and being spoken to in olde English by the very talented and dedicated actors that ran the event. But what started to turn the tide was a little bit of magic.

We were walking past a shop, when a gentleman came out and asked my girl why she was so sad. She refused to answer and then he had her take a little black crystal, hold it tight in her hands and then up to her forehead to make a wish. A wish that could come true that day, that was possible, and then once that wish came true, she had to hand the crystal off to someone else or her wish would disappear. When she opened her hands, the black crystal was now clear, and she was stunned at the magic trick.

Thankfully, she started turning around little by little. We had stopped at an oil and incense place and she even helped me pick out some of the scents. Then she got a milkshake, and you know, ice cream really does make everything better. The struggle for a smile was getting less and less, and then we happened upon a game of archery. Well both of the kids got excited—as did some of us adults—and we tried our hand at shooting arrows and being terrible at it. But there were lots of laughs all around, and then in my hand, my daughter placed her crystal. I looked at her and she said, "All I wished for was to find something fun here to do." We hugged and for the rest of the day, we were all open to the different adventures that awaited us. The shows, the yummy treats, the mead (oh hello, yummy goodness), the pirate parade and strolling through fairyland. It was all so interesting to me, and I loved every moment of it.

There was such a lightheartedness I felt inside, and I was just able to be playful and carefree in this make believe environment that I resonated so strongly with. But I think the best part was that instead of pushing my daughter to have fun, or worrying about how she was pouting, I just surrendered and let her be who she was, and feel how she felt, and it just allowed us to practice acceptance with each other. And that made for a much better day and state of mind. And of course, so did more ice cream all around at the end of a beautiful day in a magical land where I got to release my inner princess in so many ways. It was truly special.

37. A New England Escape

When I originally planned this chapter, it was supposed to be this big amazing conclusion that led to a brand new life opening. I could see it, feel it and envision exactly what I was going to say. I had even started the chapter as if it was already in existence, only needing some details from the actual experience to fill in the blanks.

Scratch that. That journey never took place, but a surprising alternative stepped in to bring everything full circle. In fact, it's rather apropos how emotionally educational this latest discovery was, considering this book was written to share the life lessons I experienced with every adventure I took, and this story certainly has multiple layers to it.

This particular weekend that I had set up to be my grand book finale, I was planning on being in San Francisco. The curiosity began about a year earlier; I kept seeing and hearing about San Francisco everywhere I went, and this lasted the entire year. The book from the author I was reading at the time was from there; a work conference I wanted to attend was there; and a woman who reached out to me to create a "real" inspirational television talk show was from there.

But the coincidences didn't end there. All over my newsfeeds, consistently I would see mention of this very city. More authors, people I met and stories came from the area. I had forgotten I had put the Golden Gate Bridge on my vision board after learning about the show opportunity, to manifest my way out there. There it was. Plain as day. All of these messages—and I mean, not a week has gone by without strong mentions of San Francisco. Even when I was trying to get out there, the synchronicities were off the chart of friends who lived out here who I could visit, other friends who just happened to be out that way that particular weekend, money-saving opportunities supporting the trip, etc. Completely insane.

I had asked the angels what this pull to go there was all about, and they had just mentioned that they wanted me to experience the energy of San Francisco—though I still had the feeling that there is something out there that awaits me. An opportunity? A relationship? It could have been anything. I wasn't quite sure what the intention for getting me out there was, but it was clear that I needed to be there. I just didn't know how.

And then I found out that the work conference I saw last year was being held there again this year, and I thought, that's it! It was the perfect opportunity to explore San Francisco while receiving new business training at the same time. It just so happened that I was researching a professional development opportunity to attend, something that was more in alignment with my skills and responsibilities than other seminars that were being offered to me, so when my computer search turned up this conference, it felt like a complete win-win, divinely orchestrated for the good of everyone.

Unfortunately, in the end, a budget cut killed that chance and I wasn't able to go. I tried to convince myself that it wasn't the right time or opportunity; that something else was meant to happen, or that I was to go there some other way, at some other time, and work just wasn't meant to be a part of it. I was open to that idea, and let go of the disappointment. The universe has a different plan, and I'd just have to wait and see what that was.

But when that trip fell through, I did immediately think, what can I write my last chapter on? How can I release the book without a significant journey? (Priorities, right?) Going to a Renaissance Faire was not all that inspirational of an ending, and my next trip to Disney really is just a repeat. But then after a conversation with my son on our front stoop, while enjoying the beautiful fall weather, talking about states he'd like to visit, it clicked—I was going to take my family on a tour of the New England states that weekend to witness the fall foliage and experience the season at its finest. As long as I had lived on Long Island, I have never done that, so I thought, what a perfect back-up plan to my San Francisco disappointment. I'm turning rotten pumpkins into pumpkin pie!

It was so perfectly planned, and something that my mother had always dreamed of, so I was surprising her with a trip of a lifetime. We were going to drive up to Vermont to see the changing colors, and enjoy a day at a resort with lots of fun fall activities. Then we'd drive through and stay in New Hampshire—just to check it off the list—before we continued our drive up into Maine. The next day, we were going to see the coast, and my mom would have her dream lobster dinner on the water.

We'd then travel down the last day to Salem, Massachusetts for a Halloween adventure, visiting the witch museum and other spooky attractions to get in the mood for the upcoming holiday. And even though we knew that would be a lot of driving, and tiring, we were ready for it! Some family bonding time, visiting states we had never been to, and proof that even when plans fall through, we can always make the best of it and choose a different adventure.

But that wasn't in the cards for us. It actually ended up being a complete disaster. Note to self: heed the mercury retrograde warnings and never plan a trip during this time (or, be prepared

> *And there it was. Clear as day. I was trying to escape. I was trying to escape the reality of my life and fill so many voids that happiness did not fill.*

for the worst). I'm not one for a GPS (I like to follow my internal one, combined with really bad mapquest directions), but after this trip, I'm sold on one. The interpretation of the directions had me looping around, thinking I was going the wrong way, only to turn back and find myself in the same spot I was in before (which was the right direction, after all), tacking on two additional hours of travel.

That wasn't that bad that it ruined the trip—yet. We got to our destination, ready to indulge in some fall festivities, but pumpkins were sold out for the pumpkin painting, the hot chocolate was awful after a half hour wait in line and not much else was going on that was all that impressive. After driving 7 hours, the kids (bless them for being such troopers though!) were like, is this it? Yeah, kids, apparently this was it. Then my daughter came down with a stomach ache, it got really cold and we starting bickering a little amongst ourselves. But we chalked it off to Vermont not being one of our favorite states, and on we went.

We started off towards our next destination: dinner and an overnight stay in New Hampshire. We were all looking forward to bed at this point. And of course, being cranky, irritable and tired of driving already, the fall foliage really held nothing special for us at that point. Sure, the scenery was beautiful, but there are only so many hours of looking at colored leaves that one can take. Perhaps if we were in a different state of mind, we would be more impressed; maybe the next day when we were in Maine, we would appreciate it again.

But when we finally arrived to New Hampshire three hours later (after more lost turns and patience wearing thin on all of our parts), we were tired and hungry and just wanted to go to sleep. We found our hotel, and a little diner near it, so we headed out to eat first. But as we were in the waiting area, I looked up my reservation to make sure I had the right hotel—and realized I had booked the wrong date. I had booked us for Sunday night there (same night I booked the Maine hotel), but not for Saturday like I was supposed to. So, I tried to keep calm and called the hotel to see if they had any availability for the night. They didn't—they were booked solid, and I couldn't switch my reservation night (but I could cancel without payment penalty, thankfully).

I tried the other 3 local hotels there, and nothing was available. Panic set in. We ordered food, but I couldn't even concentrate on that. All I cared about was trying to find a hotel anywhere along our path to stay at. But being that it was a holiday weekend, in the peak season of fall, in New England, there were no vacancies within a 4 hour radius. Not even if we skipped Maine and headed towards Massachusetts and spent more time in Salem. Absolutely nothing was available, aside from a $500 room in Boston. I wasn't about to spend that kind of money, even if it would save our trip. People in the diner were so kind and trying to help us figure out small town names, anywhere there might possibly be an open room. Phone calls were made, internet sites researched. Nothing.

It was 9pm and I didn't have a place for my children to sleep. I couldn't hold it back. I was stressed and emotional, and the tears and anger just came pouring out. This wasn't supposed to be happening. We were supposed to be on an adventure enjoying the fall, making bucket-list dreams come true. But now I was faced with the decision—argument from my mother included—to drive straight for the next 5 hours all the way home. One thing about me: when I make a decision and am determined, nothing will stop me.

I was angry. I was sad. I was beyond consolation. One child was happy the journey was coming to an end, the other showing heartbreak on his face. My mom was trying her best to switch roles; as I was the positive one on our ever-detoured trip up to Vermont, she went into over-optimistic mode during this crisis, which I was having none of. I was curt, but apologetic. I didn't want to take out my frustration on her, and I knew she had only the best intentions, but I couldn't talk about it. I just had to drive and drive and drive until I got home. It was over. I was done.

Triggered, I certainly was. I drove, trying to keep the tears from pouring down my face. I was summoning up the strength and energy to safely get my family home. I would not put their life in jeopardy, but they weren't about to sleep in a car. I'd get them home to their beds one way or another. As I demanded silence from everyone, all I could think about was, why was this happening? Why weren't the angels coming through with a backup plan? Why am I being forced to drive all the way home? Where were my options, my spark of hope?

In San Francisco. I wasn't even supposed to be here right now. I should have been in San Francisco. The anger bubbled up inside. This is not what I had wanted, or needed. I needed a break away from everything I was feeling. I was trying to escape. San Francisco fell through, so I had to fill the space with a different adventure because I just couldn't face life as it was in that moment.

And there it was. Clear as day. I was trying to escape. Unlike most other times I have gone away, where it was for the experience, this time, I was trying to escape the reality of my life and fill so many voids that happiness did not fill. I thought going on a trip around the New England states and checking off wishlist items would take away the pain of what I can't face here on Long Island. Birthday frustrations resurfaced about my job, finances and relationships, begging the deeper questions: What is my purpose? Is there such a thing? If so, am I headed in the right direction? What AM I meant to do and be? Why do I feel like I just don't belong here—or anywhere—anymore? Did I ever belong? Why even with so much healing, optimism and faith, have I been unable to make a genuine, healthy love connection?

I felt trapped in a reality that hurt my heart and soul. And the disaster of two potential escapes which were supposed to make me forget about it all, instead exposed my vulnerability and made it very, very real how I felt like a complete failure, and I wasn't sure which way to turn, or how to make it better. It left me wondering if I was on a path back to depression, and that was a scary place to be.

I realized I just couldn't cover up how I felt with a weekend getaway. Sometimes you just have to listen to your heart in your darkest moments, and hear what your inner guidance is trying to tell you, rather than fight against it. Something was intrinsically off in my life, and escaping was not the answer. I do always learn something, though, when I am out and about, and I don't intend to ever change my adventurous spirit. I just need to understand my intention behind the journeys that I do take. Some of my journeys have been directly created for healing purposes. Some of my trips were to strengthen family or friend bonds. Some had business purposes, others were for a cultural exploration. And some, like this one, were clearly a fantasy escape wishing away life as I knew it, as if I would find something better to miraculously take its place.

Not every adventure has met my expectations. But every adventure has met my needs, whether I realized it at the time or not. I can tell you this much: an adventure based on escaping from life itself is not an adventure; it is a wakeup call waiting to happen. And there is no greater lesson than awareness, because from there, you can clear out and create anew.

So what if I don't know what my life's mission or purpose is yet? I show up with the intention of being loving, helpful and supportive every day, and that is enough to inspire me to greatness. So what if I'm not exactly where I wanted to be in life yet? I'm much closer to my dreams than I was 7 years ago (or even just one year ago). So what if I don't fit in anywhere? I embrace my uniqueness, and the right people will accept me for who I am. So what if I'm not in a relationship? I have people who matter in my life who I love, and who love me. I can't force life to give me what (I think) I want, but I can choose to accept the wonderful things life <u>has</u> given me.

As for realizing that I cannot escape—the sugar-coating has been stripped away, and all I am left with is cold, hard truth. And that's the gift that I get to take away from this most recent debacle: I get to surrender and allow transformation in. I get to give up, and let life create a new adventure for me from the space that has now opened up through this clearing. I get to awaken to unlimited possibilities, and witness divinity in motion as a higher plan is revealed.

Here's my truth: The real journey is not the physical roads I travel; it is the one that is navigated within my soul.

My Escape

There's a place I seek to escape to
To take refuge from this dark
I don't know where it is
There is no map that can lead me to it
There is no "X" marks the spot
No pre-planned path to my nirvana
On a journey to the unknowns

Running away from what is
To be embraced by the what could be
All the while captured by the what was
Yearning to explore, discover, unveil truth
A desperation to change, heal, feel
Anything but here and now

My quest betrays me
A lonely adventure for one
Denying the beauty of life along the way
Traveling to anywhere
Never satisfied with any destination
Yet never wanting to return home

The journey becomes a burden
Always focused on the escape
Missing the hidden treasures

The exotics of life already in reach, but invisible and denied
Empty souvenirs
My cabinet's conquests speak of places ventured
Yet none have the brought the exquisite escape I desire

And none will until I take the ultimate trip
To one of the wonders of the world
A uniquely breathtaking destination like none other
It holds all the culture, freedom, adventure and romance I crave
All of the elements of earth, air, fire and water live here
A place of supreme harmony
Where experience and adventure wait for me
To take my breath away

Everything I've ever wanted
A dream journey that's mine for the taking
A journey to the light
A journey to peace and joy
A journey to enjoying the moment
A journey that begins now
As I simply escape to the within

Epilogue: Where to Next?

When I look back at all of the physical journeys I have taken, I myself am amazed at the profoundness of the lessons and the spiritual awakenings that have occurred. Who knew when I took my first trip to Lake George that it would begin a life-long quest of learning, healing and growing that contributed to my self-discovery? As I reflect on the common themes and challenges throughout these trips—throughout my life in general—I can feel the transformation from the young, lost girl I once was, to the strong, confident woman I have become.

It has not been an easy journey, but then again, is it for anyone? We all go through our struggles, and our experiences become part of our identities. We all have our good times, and our bad times, and never should there be a moment of regret. Do I wish some experiences were easier to go through than others? Of course I do, but there is not one experience I would change in any way. Contrast is an essential part of life. They are right when they say without knowing the helplessness of sorrow, we could not know the depths of joy. There is no pleasure without pain, no success without failure, no sun without rain, and so on. Who would want to live in a world of balanced numbness?

Not me. I choose occasional hardships so that I can relish in the gratitude of my blessings. I choose to celebrate my darkness so that my light can shine brighter.

Each one of these adventures has left a mark on my life, and each held an important lesson for me. Sometimes big, sometimes small, but each transformational in its own way. Where I "go" next is not as much physical as it is spiritual for me—though I will always boldly embrace my innate desire to explore. My time in a cocoon has certainly come to an end, and I feel the freedom of having the wings to soar in any direction I want. But I must take with me all I have learned, and honor the transformation within.

What does that mean, really? Well, first, accepting that I am a work in progress and always evolving. There will always be lessons to learn, uncovered patterns to break and challenges to test my faith and resolve. But consciously, I need to acknowledge my core beliefs, and honor myself and my values as I move forward. That's much easier said than done, as habits are so much "safer" than stepping outside of our comfort zone—even if stepping outside of our comfort zone is what is best for us.

For me, that means looking at community in a whole new light, and accepting that I am an individual who might not always fit in—but I will always make a difference. Perhaps I may truly be a serial outcast, only meant to develop one-on-one relationships and never belong to a group. And you know, that is okay with me, because I treasure the relationships that I do have, and I would never give them up for the approval of a system that I cannot—and will not—conform to.

My individuality is beautiful and unique, and I am proud to express that authentically. Not that I am not a supporter of groups, organizations, people, etc. I absolutely am, and admire them completely. My contribution to the world just does not seem to fit into that kind of a mold, and feeling like an outsider finally feels right to me.

Then there are my tumultuous relationships with men. Why are they such a recurring theme in my stories? I've become abundantly clear on my past neediness for attention and validation, and how that affected my self-esteem on multiple levels. Most likely it stems from the typical daddy issues and unrequited love stories, with a never-ending quest to just feel loved.

But now that I have made peace with the men in my life, and realized that the love for myself is stronger than any love I could receive from another, I have no space for my destructive patterns anymore. I surrender the need for external validation of my self-worth. I let go of the fear that I am unlovable exactly as I am. I accept the power of vulnerability on every level, and I will not settle for anything other than a meaningful, healthy connection. I have no better half. I am my own better half, and I need no completion.

What I do need, and want, is an equally whole partner to share my adventures with. The self-sacrifices of my past were critical to my heart and soul's opening for the right person, and I realize a few more "Mr. Wrongs" could show up along the way with more lessons to teach me—and I welcome them. But I am no longer interested in repeating the same mistakes and receiving the same messages ad nauseam. I have graduated from an elementary perspective on how love should be, and why. My new chapter has already begun—one where I trust, have faith and honor myself. And boy, does it feel good!

But it's so much more than my relationships with others. At the core, it is the relationship to myself that has needed the most tender loving care; the one that I have so long neglected. I became increasingly aware of how strong the fear has been within me. The fear of being a failure—so I quit before I was ahead. The fear of

Butterfly Travels

> *What a powerful gift to be living a dream; for in that dream for me was great transformation, wisdom and unspeakable truth.*

being rejected—so I never took a risk. The fear of not being good enough—so I put on a mask.

And then I see those very moments where I stared fear in the face, fought back, and won. How exhilarating it was for me to recall those moments—and how fulfilling! Breaking free from our own limitations is one of the most powerful forces we have within us. I have played my life way too safe, and it is time to take some risks.

It is time to remove the fears, anxieties and doubts, let myself hyperventilate as I push through the motions, and then breathe myself back to center to face the demons. I am always protected and supported by God, and if I do fail, I know that there is a deeper meaning to be revealed, or something better that is meant to be. But I cannot move forward if I stay frozen. The ice has melted, the cocoon has been busted open, and it is time to open my wings and show the world how beautiful they really are.

And I need to do so without my high standards and expectations. They really can wreak havoc on life when they aren't met. Triggered emotions, frustrations, fights—and a whole bunch of other unsavory reactions. It's okay to have a plan, but I've learned that it's much better to just go with the flow and let nature take its course. I don't need to know everything—or anything—in advance. I just have to trust myself, and my angelic guides, and I will never be led astray.

In the past, I tended to hold on way too tight to a detailed vision, and whenever something didn't work out the way I had hoped, I internalized it like a catastrophe. But the beauty of those emotions led to the discovery of how much more freedom and power there is in letting the divine take the lead. How cool is that? To not be in control, and just surrender to the flow of the universe?

It is actually perfect for a natural explorer like myself, and I have been resisting the best parts of my journeys by holding back from fully experiencing every moment. Well, no more. It's in my soul to be adventurous—and that is something I now embrace with a whole new life perspective. One that is fearless, confident and curious. One that is free, expressive and inspiring. One that is based in love, trust and faith.

So now that I have discovered the truth of who I am and what I believe, where do I want to continue my adventures? Where is my heart calling me to explore? Not to escape to—but to fuel my desire to experience the world all around me. Just thinking about it makes me feel like a kid on Christmas!!

Well, I left a part of my heart in Barcelona, and it is a dream of mine to bring my children back there one day to see where I used to live. I found that there was a Mediterranean Disney Cruise that left out of a Barcelona port which would be perfect for them. This way, they can experience a little bit of the different European cultures with me, yet still have the backup enjoyment of being spoiled by Disney fanfare. I would love to walk down my streets once more, to visit my special beach and favorite café for a hot choco-latte. And while I am in the area and the boat's cruising, I would love to check Greece off my adventure to-go list.

I definitely would like to return to Ireland, as I feel so strongly connected there. There are castles I have yet to explore, and green pastures I have yet to uncover (along with secrets—a super-sleuth never gives up on a case!) I would also love to check out my unexplored Polish heritage, and I could also give

Germany another shot—this time, I would find out where my roots specifically are and explore there. Anywhere that gives me insight into where I came from, and the history of my ancestors, is something that captivates me completely.

Hollywood has always inspired intriguing and different places to visit. A fan of the *Karate Kid* movies, I always wanted to check out Okinawa—or at the very least, Japan. I would be so jealous of my ex-husband's trips there for work, and just wished I could have traveled with him there even once. As a young girl, my very first soap opera love was *One Life to Live*, and I will never forget the scene where Tina fell over the Iguazu Falls, and ever since then (and later reinforced by the Evita movie), I've wanted to travel to Argentina to see them.

Australia is another "to see" place, as I am so intrigued by the accents, culture and apparent hospitality. And I think it would be cool to see an authentically-living koala bear munching on a eucalyptus leaf! Going on an African safari would also be absolutely amazing, as would a trip to Mexico and Bali.

But number one on my list, hands down, is Egypt. I feel as strong a connection there as I do to Ireland; perhaps more so. As a child, I was completely fascinated with pyramids, the story of Cleopatra and hieroglyphics. Those especially were curious for me. As I grew older, my favorite Broadway show became Aida, and I just couldn't get enough of it. I understand that modern-day Egypt is extremely dangerous for young American women, but I will not give up hope that one day I will be there, able to freely explore a country I know has deep-rooted meaning for me yet to be revealed. No doubt, connected to a past life of mine.

I am sure I am missing a few foreign places I want to go to, and I will get around to all of it one day. Of that, I have no doubt. But for now, my exploratory focus is on the United States, and one of the biggest adventures of my life: a double cross-country trip. I know—my long drive through New England was not the best experience, and you would think it would be an indication of what it would be like to actually do these long kinds of road trips (and steer clear of them). But, no can do. I have an adventure list to check off! (And a GPS to purchase.)

My intention is to hit as many states as possible on these journeys, and really get a taste of how different the cultures are even within my own country. There are so many amazing people I would love to see across the States, and that experience alone is so much more meaningful than seeing some colorful fall trees. How could I resist a trip where I get to deepen so many special connections in my life? It's an opportunity that may never come my way again, and it is something I have always wanted to do ever since hearing stories about my grandparent's cross-country road trip.

They are the ones who inspired me to be adventuresome and go exploring. I owe that streak in me to them, and to my children who continue to encourage and inspire my inner child. I owe my many lessons, both loving and hurtful, to so many wonderful people I have met along these different paths, and I am forever grateful for their presence in my life, whether reason, season or lifetime. I owe feeling and knowing that at the end of it all, there truly is no place like home, to my family, most of all, my mom, who gave me a great foundation. And I owe these opportunities to take risks and explore life to its fullest to God and the universe, and to myself for accepting them.

What a powerful gift to be living a dream; for in that dream for me has been great transformation, wisdom and unspeakable truth. Truth that no matter where I go, I am always me, and am I here on this earth to experience, to love, to flourish and to discover.

Perhaps these physical adventures are the catalyst for many an awakening; but it is the spiritual awakenings that walk hand in hand with the physical that have revealed the woman—the soul—that I am inside. And it is that journey within that has been the greatest adventure of all.

"Just when the caterpillar thought the world was over, it became a butterfly."

~ Proverb

About the Author

Jennifer Watson, MS, CTACC, is a writer, speaker and international promoter of love and triumph. As a certified life coach, she provides a unique blend of coaching and self empowerment techniques designed to encourage clients to break through their blocks and embrace their power…after breaking down their pity parties. She's also the online personality of her weekly youtube show, *Confessions*, where she gets deep into the hearts of inspirational guests to reveal their transformational journeys, plus interviews expert panelists to expose the darkness of uncomfortable topics to bring important issues to light.

Jennifer has been in the marketing/communications field for over 17 years, where she gained a rich, diverse professional experience and strong business sense that later served as the foundation of her entrepreneurialism. An avid writer since childhood, her career in professional writing and ongoing personal and guest blogging anchored her passion and encouraged her dream to become an author—and from there, her first book, *Butterfly Travels*, was born.

Embrace Your Power ~ *www.jennifer-watson.me*

About the Illustrator

Special thanks to my wonderful illustrator—and friend—Elizabeth Hamby, for her beautiful artwork. I had a vision, and she captured it perfectly and poetically with her gifts. If you are interested in her custom illustrations, please reach out to her at *rowangrovecreations@gmail.com*.

www.ingramcontent.com/pod-product-compliance
Lightning Source LLC
Chambersburg PA
CBHW061322040426
42444CB00011B/2738